KAREN BROWN'S

Italian
Country Bed & Breakfasts

OTHER KAREN BROWN TITLES

Austrian Country Inns & Castles

California Country Inns & Itineraries

English Country Bed & Breakfasts

English, Welsh & Scottish Country Hotels & Itineraries

French Country Bed & Breakfasts

French Country Inns & Itineraries

German Country Inns & Itineraries

Irish Country Inns

Italian Country Bed & Breakfasts

Italian Country Inns & Itineraries

Portuguese Country Inns & Pousadas

Scandinavian Country Inns & Manors

Spanish Country Inns & Paradors

Swiss Country Inns & Chalets

KAREN BROWN'S

Italian
Country Bed & Breakfasts

Written by

NICOLE FRANCHINI

Sketches and Cover

by

Elisabetta Franchini

Karen Brown's Country Inn Series

Editors: Karen Brown, Clare Brown, June Brown
Iris Sandilands, Cynthia Sauvage, Nicole Franchini
Technical support: William H. Brown III

Illustrations and cover painting: Elisabetta Franchini
Maps: Cassell Design

This book is written in cooperation with:
Town and Country - Hillsdale Travel, San Mateo, CA 94401

Copyright © 1992 by Karen Brown's Guides

Distributed by
The Globe Pequot Press, 138 West Main Street, Chester, CT 06412

Library of Congress Cataloging-in-Publication Data

Franchini, Nicole, 1959
    Karen Brown's Italian country bed & breakfasts/ written by Nicole
Franchini ; sketches & cover by Elisabetta Franchini.
      p.   cm. -- (Karen Brown's country inn series)
    Includes index.
    ISBN 0-930328-06-X (pbk.)
    1. Bed and breakfast accommodations--Italy--Guide-books.
2. Italy--Description and travel--1975- --Guide-books. I. Brown,
Karen. II. Title III. Title: Italian country bed & breakfasts.
IV. Title: Italian country bed & breakfasts. V. Series
TX907.5.I8F73 1992
647.944503--dc20
                        91-75266
                        CIP

For my inherited passion of all things Italian,

I dedicate this book to Papa,

and In loving memory of Mother

ACKNOWLEDGEMENTS

I wish to thank the following persons whose invaluable
assistance was fundamental in the realization of this guide:

First and foremost to Dott. Giorgio Medici, General Secretary Anagritur
for his tremendous support and limitless enthusiasm

Dott. Giorgio LoSurdo, Director Agriturist

Dott.ssa Livia Pianelli, National Secretary Terranostra

Antonella Lazzareschi, Agriturist Firenze

Dott. Massimo Bartolelli, Prof. University of Bari

Dott. Pompeo Braccio, Regional Director Federation of Puglia

Giuseppe, Carmelo and Sandra; University of Bari & Tecnagro

Giorgio and Elli Bianchi, Podere Val delle Corti, Radda in Chianti

Emanuele De Ferrari, La Dogana, Tuoro sul Trasimeno

Antonino Puglisi, technical support

Carlo Angelini

Cristina Giorgetti and Mauro Mortaroli

My ever-supportive siblings Alessandro, Luisa and Elisabetta,
who took time between shows to produce the artwork for the guide

All the B&B hosts and hostesses who welcomed me into their homes
and to their dinner tables

AND, MOST IMPORTANTLY, MY THANKS TO THE FARMERS OF ITALY

Nicole Franchini, author

Foreword

We are pleased to present *Italian Country Bed & Breakfasts*, the latest addition to our country inn series. This is the first guide book written that features bed and breakfast accommodations in Italy. *Agriturismo*, as the bed and breakfast activity is called in Italy, has made great strides over the past decade. The B&B concept is relatively new to Italy, which followed suit after France and England originated the trend. To bring you this personal selection of places to stay, tens of thousands of country-road kilometers have been traveled, and hundreds of B&Bs inspected. Accommodations vary from simple farmhouses to noble country villas, all promising unique and memorable stays. For the first-time or the return visitor, an agriturismo vacation offers the superb opportunity to interact directly with Italians, experiencing their way of life as a participant rather than just an observer.

ITALIAN FARMER'S POEM

Our memories are crouched
in silence within the belly of the earth.
Yet it takes only a day of sunshine,
an impromtu storm in the sky,
the perfume of freshly cut hay,
and immense fields dotted with golden haystacks,
to ignite in us the memories
of certain evenings spent full of gaiety.

It was at sunset when we used to join together
in the barn filled with grain
to celebrate the end of the harvest.
The "gioanassa" musician friend,
pressing the keys of his worn-out accordian,
succeeding in emitting the notes
to a waltz or mazurka, leaving us
drunk with happiness.

One more glass of wine before the night
fades into day.
One more toast to bid farewell
to another summer
that crossed the path of our youth.

--Anonymous

Contents

Introduction

BED AND BREAKFAST ITALIAN-STYLE: Agritourism travel offers visitors to Italy the unique opportunity to observe daily life as a guest in someone's home. This loose organization most closely resembles a network of bed-and-breakfast-type accommodations offering a more intimate contact with the country's traditional ways of life than can be experienced during hotel stays. It is the alternative vacation for curious visitors who wish to explore the back roads of this fascinating country and depart with a more in-depth understanding of Italians and their lifestyles than they could possibly acquire from city stays and sightseeing alone. The individual who will benefit most from agritourism will have an open, inquiring mind and a certain amount of flexibility. In return, agritourism rewards the traveler with a feeling of being at home abroad. The warm welcome and the value you'll receive may bring you back to the agritourism track year after year.

Called *agriturismo* in Italian, this term, defined as agricultural tourism, was founded as a national association in 1965, in part by the Italian government. Its objective was to make it possible for farmers to supplement their declining income in two ways: by offering accommodations to tourists and by direct sales of their produce.

After World War II, during reconstruction and the subsequent industrial boom, Italians abandoned the countryside in droves in search of employment in urban centers, reducing the rural population from eight- to three-million people. Consequently, farmhouses, villas and castles all across the country were neglected and went to ruin. This phenomenon also disrupted the centuries-old tradition of passing customs and property from one generation to the next.

The agritourism concept, with its government funding and proclaimed tax breaks, has lured proprietors back to their land and ancestral homes, providing them with the incentive to restore and preserve these wonderful historical buildings (there are many treasures among them), without spoiling the natural beauty of the landscape. An additional consequence is an improved distribution of tourism between Italy's overcrowded cities and the countryside, serving to raise awareness of the many marvelous attractions, from art and architecture to scenery and cuisine, that await tourists off the beaten track. Each of Italy's 20 regions participates in agritourism, with a full 60% of participants concentrated in Tuscany and Trentino Alto Adige. In this first edition of *Italian Country Bed & Breakfasts,* selections from 12 regions have been included.

In practical terms, agritourism was developed to stimulate the economy in rural areas. By encouraging the creation of accommodation (rooms, apartments and campgrounds) in places where they had never before been available, the government hoped to stimulate local economies. In a more long-term and idealistic sense, it was hoped that the promotion and development of tourism in rural Italy would also bring about greater environmental awareness and rescue traditional folklore and customs, such as regional cuisine and handicrafts, from oblivion and for posterity.

For Italians, agritourism facilitates an exchange of views between farmers and urbanites who come in search of a peaceful vacation surrounded by natural beauty. In fact, agritourism and the rich culture of the farmer represent for some an affirmation and validation of their heritage. Lamentably, some Italians have a misconception of agritourism because it was originally organized as an exchange of very basic room and board for work in the fields. Even though this is no longer the case, there remains today an unfortunate lack of awareness of the variety of accommodations (from simple farmhouse to elaborate castle) available through the associations. Hence, the activity has not flourished to its potential.

Controversy also surrounds the fact that there are few established regulations governing this type of activity, and they differ greatly from one region to another. Consequently, no clearly defined quality standard exists and those participants with limited economic resources resent wealthier proprietors, whom they accuse of running accommodations more resembling hotels than farm stays. Moreover, it doesn't simplify matters that agritourism is organized in typical Italian fashion, with responsibility divided among three associations, each with its own regulations, politics and guidelines. Each produces a directory (in Italian), and may be contacted by writing to:

AGROTIROST, Corso Vittorio Emanuele 101, Rome 00168, Italy

TERRANOSTRA, Via XIV Maggio 43, Rome 00187, Italy

TURSSMO VERDE, Via M. Fortuny 20, Rome 00196, Italy

ACCOMMODATIONS

DESCRIPTIONS: The B&Bs in this guide are described in terms of the criteria used in their selection: warmth of hospitality offered, historic character and charm of the homes, surrounding scenery, proximity to sites of touristic interest, and the quality of the cuisine. Obviously, all of these attributes are not always found in each B&B - read the description carefully to choose a place to stay best suited to you. Agritourism accommodations should not be thought of strictly in terms of the English definition of B&B, as they vary greatly according to each proprietor's interpretation of the concept.

FOOD: A highlight of the agritourism experience is without a doubt the food. Most travelers would agree that a bad meal is hard to find in Italy, a country world-famous for its culinary skills. In the countryside you'll be sampling the traditional recipes from which Italian cuisine originates. Because, whenever possible, all of the ingredients come directly from the farms where you'll be staying, you'll discover the flavorful difference freshness can make. A peek into the farm kitchen is likely to reveal pasta being rolled and cut the old old-fashioned way: by hand. Many country cooks prefer preparing food using traditional methods, not relying on machines to speed up the process.

LANGUAGE: The English spoken at each B&B has been indicated as follows: fluent, very well, well, some, little or none. In any case, it is helpful (not to mention rewarding) to have a few basic Italian phrases at hand. A phrase book or dictionary is indispensable.

LENGTH OF STAY: Agritourism is most advantageous for those who have more than the standard two weeks to travel. B&B accommodations take longer to reach, for one thing, plus often they're neither set up nor staffed for one-night stays, which increase costs and defeat the purpose. There are numerous exceptions, however, especially in B&Bs near cities, where overnight guests are accepted. Where a minimum stay is required it has been noted in the description. Another option is two- or three-bedroom apartment-suites within homes, available for those wishing to stay in one place for at least a week. They usually include a living/eating area plus kitchenette, and, except in rare occasions, the room rate does not include breakfast.

MEALS OFFERED: B&Bs sometimes serve breakfast only - usually consisting of a choice of coffee or tea, freshly-baked breads and home-made jams. However, many prepare other meals, as well, and offer (sometimes require) half- or full-board plans to guests. Half board means that breakfast and dinner are both included in the daily per-person room rate. Full board rate includes the room and all three meals and is less common; most guests are out and about during the day, or prefer one lighter meal. Dinner is a hearty three-course meal, often shared at a common table with the host family, and usually includes wine. Menus might be set daily according to the availability of fresh produce, or a limited choice may be given. Other times a farm will have a full-fledged restaurant serving non-guests as well. So that travelers who are not necessarily guests at a particular B&B may take advantage of this opportunity to sample other fare, B&Bs with restaurants are distinguished by the term "All meals served". It is advisable to reserve in advance. "Trattoria on premises" indicates a restaurant which exists as a separate function to the B&B.

RATES: Room rates vary according to size, season and level of service and luxury. Rates range from $50 to $180 for a double room with breakfast (indicated as B&B in the following descriptions) and from $35 to $100 per person for room with half board (half board includes breakfast and dinner). The majority of the B&Bs selected for this guide have private bathrooms. Approximate prices for 1992 are indicated in lire. Rates include tax and breakfast unless otherwise indicated, and are confirmed upon reservation. Credit cards are rarely accepted, cash being the preferred method of payment. When "plastic payment" is taken, the type of card accepted will be indicated as follows: AX=American Express; VS=Visa; MC=Master Card; DC=Diner's Club; or all major. Because of its cost advantages, agritourism is an ideal choice for a family vacation. Children under eight are usually offered a discount and hosts will almost always add an extra bed for a small charge.

RESERVATIONS: Whether you plan to stay in several B&Bs or decide to remain for an extended period at just one, advance reservations are needed. Not only do many of the B&Bs have only a few bedrooms available, but also they are usually in private homes that are not prepared to take walk-in traffic. There are several ways to make a reservation:

Fax: A few places to stay (especially in or near cities) have fax numbers. Faxing is a quick way to make a reservation (remember to include your fax number for their response).

Mail: You can write to the B&B (allow up to 6 weeks for an answer because mail to Italy is very slow).   If you have plenty of time and decide to write, make photocopies of the sample reservation-request letter (page 161) written in Italian with an English translation.   (Note: In correspondence, be sure to spell out the month.)   Frequently a deposit is requested in order to confirm the reservation.

Reservation service: If you want to pay for the convenience of having the reservations made for you, prepayments made and vouchers issued, any of the B&Bs in this guide can be booked through *Hidden Treasures of Italy* a booking service run by the author of this guide, Nicole Franchini.   Further information as to the charges and the request form are found in the back of this book.

Telephone: You can call the B&B directly.   This is very efficient since you will get an immediate response.   (The level of English spoken is given in each B&B description).   To telephone Italy from the United States, dial 011 (the international code), then 39 (Italy's code), then the city code (dropping the 0), and the telephone number.   Allow for the time difference in Italy which is 6 hours ahead of New York.

Travel agent: You can ask your travel agent to assist you with your reservations. Be aware that most travel agents will charge for their services since it is time consuming to make reservations and most places to stay in this guide are too small to pay any commission to compensate for the costs involved.

TYPE OF SERVICE: The most important thing to remember as you consider an agritourism vacation is that you will be staying in the *private homes* of families that are obligated to run their B&Bs without hiring additional personnel aside from family and farmhands.   Do not forget that, in most cases, the primary responsibility of your hosts is the running of their farm.   So, with a few noted exceptions, do not expect the service of a hotel.   Nevertheless, do anticipate a comfortable and enjoyable stay, because the proprietors will do everything possible to assure it. Cost will vary according to the level of service offered. (For the traveler's convenience, some city hotels have been included that are similar to a B&B in style, but go by the name Albergo, Pensione or Hotel.)

WHAT TO SEE AND DO: B&B proprietors take pride in their farms and great pleasure in answering questions about their agricultural activity. They will often take time to explain and demonstrate procedures such as wine making, olive pressing or cheese production. They will also be happy to suggest local itineraries, including historic sites, picturesque villages and cultural activities. Your B&B hosts are an incomparable resource for information about the surrounding area - don't hesitate to seek their advice. You'll discover that some owners organize weekly courses in language, cooking and handicrafts. In addition, many B&B hosts feel responsible for entertaining their guests and have added swimming pools or tennis courts if they are not already available in the vicinity. Other activities such as archery, fishing, hiking and biking are sometimes offered. Horseback riding has made an enormous comeback and farms frequently have their own stables and organize lessons and/or excursions into the countryside.

Introduction

BANKS

Banking hours are Monday through Friday from 8:30 to 1:30 and 3:00 to 4:00. *Cambio* signs outside and inside a bank indicate that it will exchange traveler's checks or give you cash from certain credit cards.

DRIVING IN ITALY

DRIVER'S LICENSE: An overseas driver's license is valid for driving throughout Italy, which is not *quite* the vehicular free-for-all you may have heard about, at least not outside big cities (particularly Rome, Florence and Milan). When visiting Rome, it's advisable to do so at the beginning or end of your trip before you pick up or after you drop off your car. Italians have a different relationship with the basic rules of the road. Common maneuvers include running stop lights and stop signs, triple parking, driving 160 kph on the highways and passing on the right. But once out of the city, you will find it relatively easy to reach your destination. Road directions are quite good in Italy.

DISTANCES: Distances are indicated in kilometers (km), one km equals 0.621 miles. Km can be roughly calculated into miles by cutting the km distance in half. Distances between towns are shown in orange alongside the roads on the Touring Club maps. Italy is a compact country and distances are relatively short, yet you will be amazed at how dramatically the scenery can change within an hour's drive.

GAS COUPONS: Foreigners often are confused about gas coupons (maybe because the rules change every six months or so). Available only to tourists, these coupons can be purchased at national borders and from the automobile club of Italy (ACI) upon arrival at either the Milan or Rome airport. The savings are up to 20% and include tollway vouchers and free breakdown service. Coupons can be refunded at the place of purchase. Packets are sold according to your area of destination: north, central or south Italy.

GASOLINE - PRICES: Gas prices in Italy are the highest in Europe, and

Americans often suspect a mistake when their first fill up comes to $40 to $60 (most of it taxes).   Some stations now accept Visa credit cards, and the ERG stations accept American Express.   Besides the AGIP stations on the autostrade, which are almost always open, gas stations observe the same hours as merchants, closing in the afternoon from 12:30 to 4:00 and in the evening at 7:30.   Be careful not to get caught running on empty in the afternoon!   Many stations have a self-service pump which operates on off-hours, and accepts *only* 10,000-lire bills.   *Warning:* At tollway gas stations and snack bars, always lock your car and beware of gypsies and vendors who try to sell you stolen merchandise.   In general, never leave valuables in the car.

MAPS: An above-average map of Italy is absolutely essential for this type of travel.   The Touring Club Italiano maps, in an easy-to-read three-volume format divided into North, Central and South, is a superior selection.   Even the smallest town is indicated in the extensive index.   In addition, places of particular interest are underlined or boxed in green, as are exceptionally scenic roads.   The Rand McNally Hallwag maps are a fine choice.   Depending upon your itinerary, you need either their map of "Northern Italy" or "Southern Italy," or both (the whole-country map isn't specific enough).   Each comes with a small index booklet to help you find the towns you are seeking.

ROADS: Names of roads in Italy are as follows:

Autostrada: Autostrade are a direct and convenient way to cover long distances. These two- or three-lane tollways are marked by green signs bearing an "A" followed by the autostrada number.   Speed limit: 130 kph.

Superstrada: A one- or two-lane freeway between secondary cities marked by blue signs and given a number.   Speed limit: 110 kph.

Strada statale: A small one-lane road marked with S.S. followed by the road number.

Raccordo or *tangenziale:*   A ring road around cities, connecting to autostrade.

ROAD SIGNS: Yellow signs are for tourists and indicate a site of historical or cultural interest, hotels and restaurants. Black-and-yellow signs indicate the name and location of private companies and industries.

TOLLS: Tolls on Italian autostrade are quite steep, ranging from $15 to $20 for a three-hour stretch, but offering the fastest and most direct way to travel between cities. Fortunately for the agritourist traveler, tollways are rarely necessary. However, if it suits your needs, a *viacard,* or magnetic reusable card for tolls, is available in all tollway gas stations for 50,000 or 90,000 lire (the lines for the machines taking these cards are always shortest).

FARM PRODUCE

You will be enticed by the products offered for sale at the farms such as wines, virgin olive oil, jams and honeys, cheese and salami, along with local artisans' handicraft. U.S. customs allows residents to bring in $400 worth of goods duty-free (including 2 bottles of liquor), after which a straight 10% duty is levied. The import of fresh cheese, meat or produce is forbidden unless it is vacuum-packed.

FINDING YOUR B&B

Directions to help you find your destination are given after each B&B description. The beauty of many of these B&Bs is that they are off the beaten track, but that characteristic may also make them tricky to find. If you get lost, first keep your sense of humor, then call the proprietors and/or ask locals at bars or gas stations for directions. As previously mentioned, detailed maps for the area in which you will be traveling are essential to supplement the maps given in this guide.

For reference, the 20 regions of Italy from north to south are as follows: *North -* Valle d'Aosta, Liguria, Piedmont, Friuli Veneto Giulia, Trentino Alto Adige, Lombardy, Veneto and Emilia-Romagna. *Central -* Tuscany, Umbria, The Marches, Lazio, Abruzzo and Molise. *South -* Campania, Apulia, Calabria, Basilicata, Sicily and Sardinia. Provinces indicated in addresses and on license plates are:

AL Alessandria	AN Ancona	AR Arezzo	AP Ascoli Piceno
AT Asti	BA Bari	BL Belluno	BG Bergamo
BO Bologna	BZ Bolzano	BS Brescia	BR Brindisi
CO Como	FI Firenze	OF Forli	GE Genova
GR Grosseto	LU Lucca	MN Mantova	MI Milano
MO Modena	NA Napoli	NO Novara	PD Padova
PR Parma	PV Pavia	PG Perugia	PS Pesaro
PI Pisa	PT Pistoia	RA Ravenna	SI Siena
TA Taranto	TR Terni	TO Torino	TN Trento
TV Treviso	VE Venezia	VC Vercelli	VR Verona
VI Vicenza	VT Viterbo		

It is important to know that addresses in the countryside often have no specific street name, let alone number. A common address consists of the farm name, sometimes a *localita* (an unincorporated area, or vicinity, frequently not found on a map) and the town name followed by the province abbreviated in parentheses. The B&B is not necessarily in that town, but it serves as a post office reference.

The localita can also be the name of the road and is often your best clue as to where the B&B is located.

GLOSSARY OF FARM NAMES

The following names for farms, seen throughout this guide, vary from area to area.

AZIENDA AGRICOLA - a general term meaning farm, not necessarily offering hospitality
BORGO - a small stone-walled village usually of medieval origins
CASALE & CASOLARE - variations of "farmhouse", deriving from "casa"
CASCINA & CA'- farm in Piedmont, Lombardy and Veneto
FATTORIA & PODERE - typically a farm in Tuscany or Umbria
HOF & MASO - terms meaning house and farm in the northern mountain areas
LOCANDA - historically a restaurant with rooms for travelers passing through on horseback
MASSERIA - fortified farms in Apulia
POGGIO - literally describes the farm's position on a flat hilltop
TENUTA - estate
TORRE - tower
TRATTORIA - a simple, family-run restaurant in cities and the countryside
VILLA & CASTELLO - usually former home of nobility and more elaborate in services

PLANNING YOUR TRIP

INFORMATION: The Italian Government Travel Offices (ENIT) can offer general information on various regions and their cultural attractions. They cannot offer specific information on restaurants and accommodations. Offices are located in the United States and Canada at:

CHICAGO: 500 N. Michigan Ave., Chicago, IL 60011; (312) 644-0990

NEW YORK: 630 5th Ave., Ste. 1565, New York, NY 10111; (212) 245-4822

SAN FRANCISCO: 360 Post Street, San Francisco, CA 94108; (415) 392-6206

MONTREAL: 3 Place Ville Marie, Montreal, Quebec, Canada; (514) 866-7667

PERIOD OF TRAVEL: Since agritourism accommodations are usually within permanent residences, many remain open all year, while others are open typically from Easter through November. If you are traveling outside this time, however, it is worth a phone call to find out if the B&B will accommodate you anyway. The best time for agritourism traveling is without a doubt during the spring and fall months, when nature is in its glory. You can witness the *vendemia,* or grape harvest, at the end of September, the flowers blossoming in May, or olive-oil production and truffle hunts in November and December. Southern Italy can be mild and pleasant in the winter, which might be perfect for travelers who like to feel they are the only tourists around. The vast majority of Italians vacation during the month of August, Easter weekend and Christmas, so these time periods are best avoided, if possible.

SHOPPING

Italy is a shopper's paradise. Not only are the stores brimming with tempting merchandise, but the displays are works of art. From the tiniest fruit market to the most chic boutique, the owners take great pride in making their shops places of beauty. Each region seems to specialize in something. In Venice handblown glass and handmade lace are popular. Milan is famous for its clothing and silk. Florence is a center for leathergoods and gold jewelry. Rome is a fashion hub, where you can stroll the pedestrian shopping streets and browse in some of the world's most elegant shops boasting the latest designer creations. Religious items are also plentiful in Rome, particularly near St Peter's Cathedral. Naples and the surrounding area (Capri, Ravello and Positano) offer delightful coral jewelry and also a wonderful selection of ceramics. Many areas outside the metropolitan centers are well-reputed for certain handicrafts; ask your B&B host about local artisans's work.

TELEPHONES

The Italian phone company (the infamous SIP) has been an object of ridicule, a source of frustration and a subject of heated conversation since its inception; and rightfully so.   Over half of the phone calls initiated are never completed.   It is one of most archaic and inefficient communication systems in existence in the developed world.   To make matters at least not any worse, keep the following in mind (and be prepared to "try, try again").   To make a call within Italy, always dial the "0" before the area code; from outside Italy, the "0" is eliminated.   Be aware that no warning is given when the time you've paid for is about to expire (the line just goes dead) - so put in plenty of change (unused coins will be refunded).

There are several types of phones (in various stages of modernization) in Italy:
Gray phones are best for local calls.   These take *gettoni,* or tokens, which are available at bars and tobacco stores for 200 lire.

Regular rotary phones in bars, restaurants and many B&Bs, which you can use *a scatti,* meaning you can pay the proprietor after the call is completed.

Bright orange pay phones which accept 500-, 200- and 100-lire coins as well as *gettoni.*

Bright orange pay phones with attached apparatus permitting insertion of a *scheda telefonica,* or reusable magnetic card worth 5,000 or 10,000 lire.

To call the United States, matters have been eased by the ongoing installation of the Country Direct System, whereby with one 200-lire coin you can reach an American operator by dialing either 172-1011 for AT&T or 172-1022 for MCI. Either a collect call or a credit-card call can then be placed.   If you discover this system doesn't work from some smaller towns, dial 170 to place a collect call, or try dialing direct (from a *scatti* phone), using the international code 001 + area code + number.

TRANSPORTATION

A car is a must for this type of travel. Most B&Bs are inaccessible by any other means of transportation. A car gives the traveler a great deal of independence (public transportation is frequently on strike in Italy), plus it provides the ideal means with which to explore the countryside thoroughly. Rental cars are readily available at all the commercial airports and in all major cities. It is best to reserve a vehicle and prepay before your departure to insure the best rates possible.

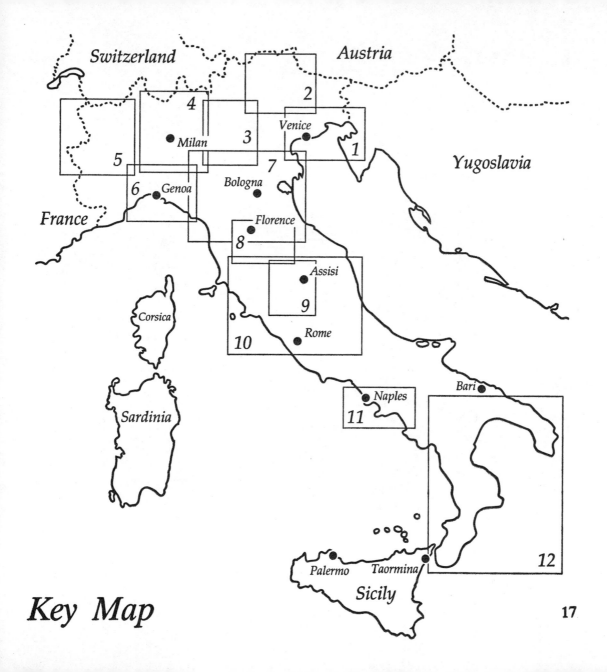

Switzerland

Austria

2

4

3

Venice

1

Milan

Yugoslavia

5

7

6 Genoa

Bologna

France

Florence

8

Corsica

Assisi

9

Rome

10

Sardinia

Bari

Naples

11

12

Palermo   Taormina

Sicily

Key Map

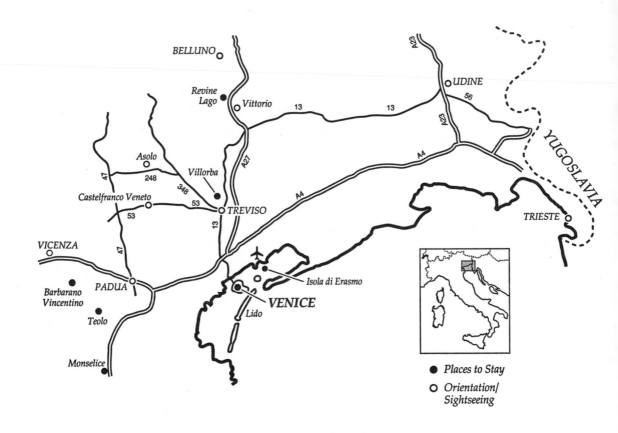

BELLUNO ○

Revine ● Lago

Vittorio ○

13   13

UDINE ○

56

A23

A23

A4

YUGOSLAVIA

Asolo ○

248

Villorba ●

A27

348

A4

TRIESTE ○

Castelfranco Veneto ○

53

53

13

○ TREVISO

47

VICENZA ○

47

Barbarano
Vincentino ●

PADUA ○

Teolo ●

Isola di Erasmo

VENICE

Lido

Monselice ●

● *Places to Stay*

○ *Orientation/*
  Sightseeing

Map 1

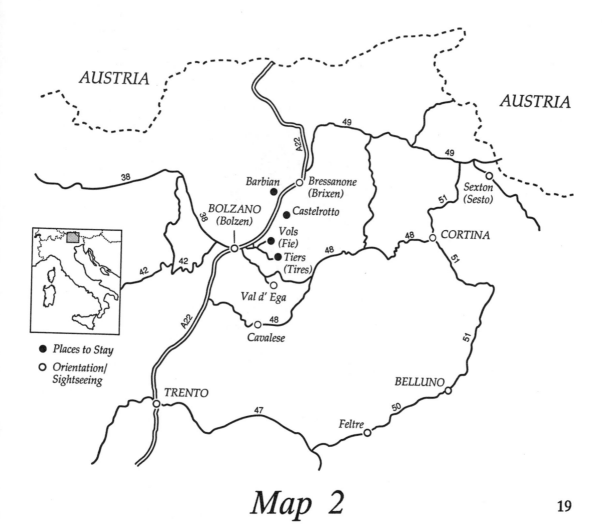

AUSTRIA

AUSTRIA

38

A22

49

49

Barbian

Bressanone
(Brixen)

Sexton
(Sesto)

BOLZANO
(Bolzen)

Castelrotto

51

38

Vols
(Fie)

48

CORTINA

42

42

Tiers
(Tires)

48

51

● *Places to Stay*

○ *Orientation/
Sightseeing*

Val d' Ega

48

51

A22

Cavalese

BELLUNO

TRENTO

50

47

Feltre

Map 2

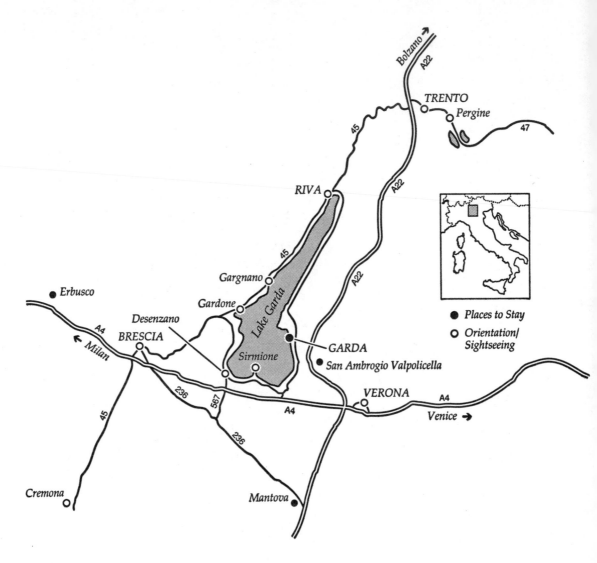

Map 3

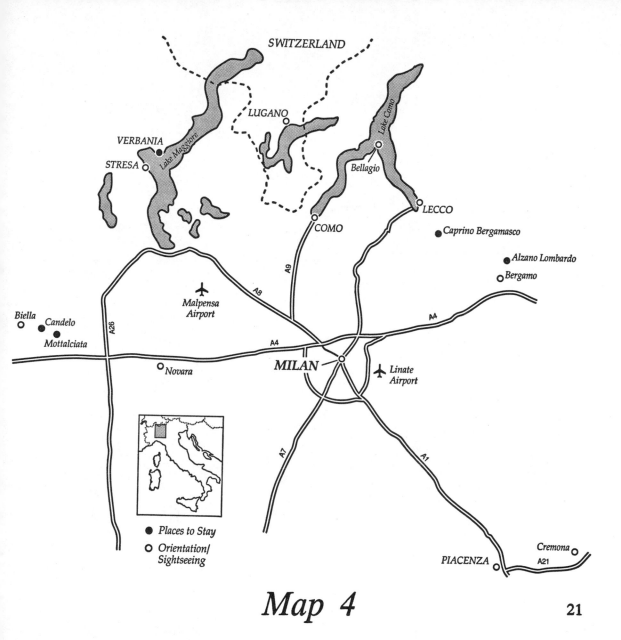

SWITZERLAND

LUGANO

Lake Como

VERBANIA

Lake Maggiore

STRESA

Bellagio

LECCO

● Caprino Bergamasco

COMO

A9

● Alzano Lombardo

○ Bergamo

✈
Malpensa
Airport

A8

A4

Biella ○
● Candelo
● Mottalciata

A26

A4

○ Novara

MILAN ○

✈ Linate
Airport

A7

A1

● *Places to Stay*

○ *Orientation/
Sightseeing*

PIACENZA ○

Cremona ○

A21

Map 4

21

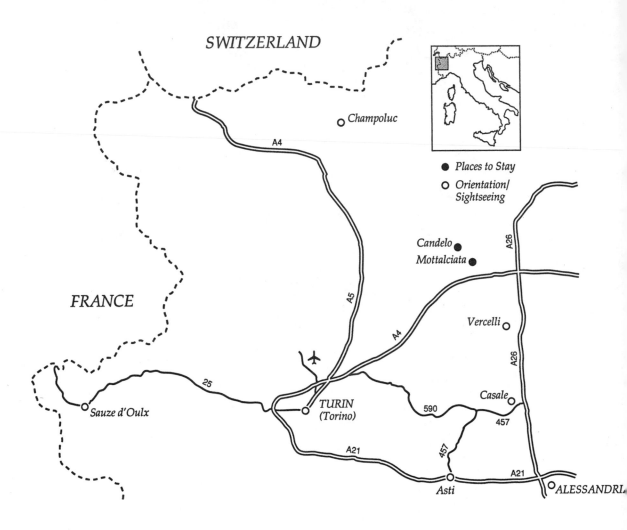

SWITZERLAND

○ Champoluc

A4

FRANCE

A5

A4

A26

Candelo ●
Mottalciata ●

● Places to Stay
○ Orientation/
   Sightseeing

Vercelli ○

A26

25

TURIN
(Torino)

590

Casale ○

○ Sauze d'Oulx

A21

457

457

Asti ○

A21

○ ALESSANDRI

22

Map 5

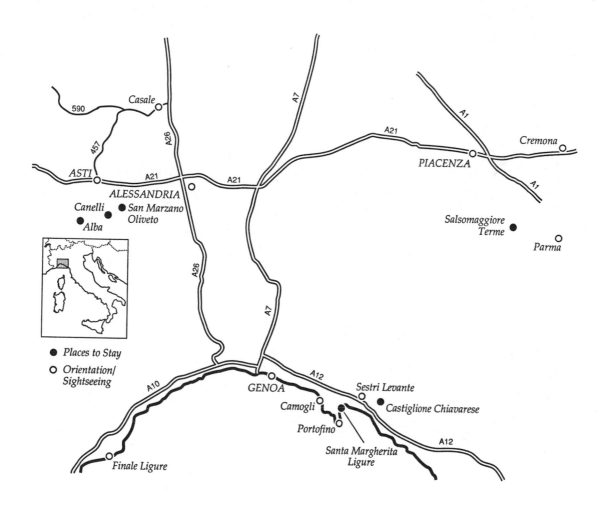

Map 6

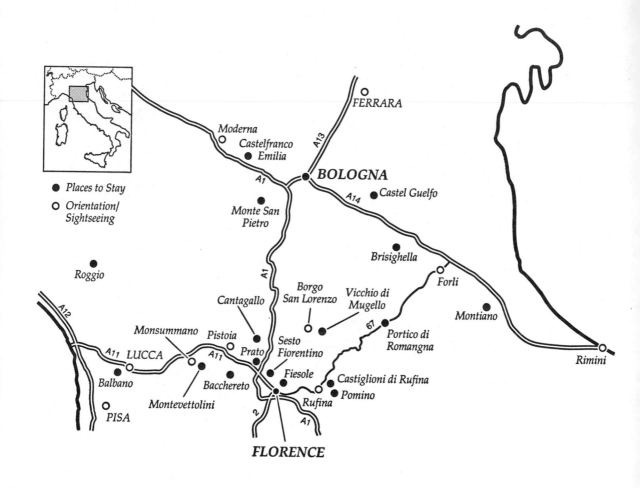

Map 7

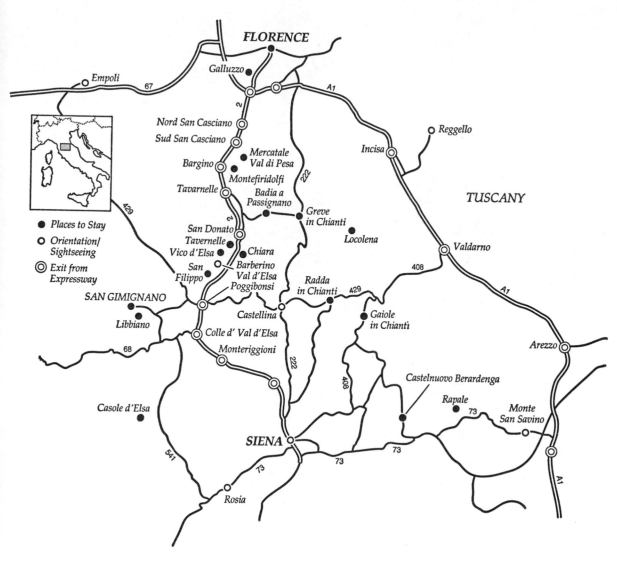

Places to Stay

○ **Orientation/Sightseeing**

◎ **Exit from Expressway**

FLORENCE

Galluzzo

Empoli

Nord San Casciano

Sud San Casciano

Bargino

Mercatale Val di Pesa

Tavarnelle

Montefiridolfi

Badia a Passignano

San Donato Tavernelle

Greve in Chianti

Vico d'Elsa

Chiara

San Filippo

Barberino Val d'Elsa

Poggibonsi

SAN GIMIGNANO

Libbiano

Castellina

Colle d' Val d'Elsa

Monteriggioni

Casole d'Elsa

SIENA

Rosia

Reggello

Incisa

TUSCANY

Valdarno

Locolena

Radda in Chianti

Gaiole in Chianti

Arezzo

Castelnuovo Berardenga

Rapale

Monte San Savino

Map 8

25

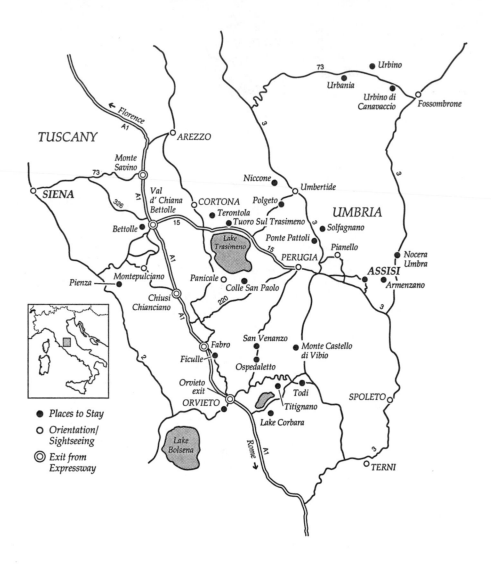

TUSCANY

← Florence
A1

AREZZO

Monte
Savino

73

A1

SIENA

326

Val
d' Chiana
Bettolle

CORTONA

Bettolle

15

Niccone

Umbertide

Polgeto

UMBRIA

Terontola

Tuoro Sul Trasimeno

Solfagnano

3

Lake
Trasimeno

Ponte Pattoli

Pianello

15

Montepulciano

PERUGIA

Nocera
Umbra

Pienza

Panicale

Colle San Paolo

ASSISI

Armenzano

Chiusi
Chianciano

A1

220

3

San Venanzo

2

Fabro

Monte Castello
di Vibio

Ficulle

Ospedaletto

Orvieto
exit

Todi

SPOLETO

ORVIETO

Titignano

Lake Corbara

Places to Stay

Orientation/
Sightseeing

Lake
Bolsena

Rome
A1

Exit from
Expressway

3

TERNI

73

Urbino

Urbania

Urbino di
Canavaccio

Fossombrone

3

Map 9

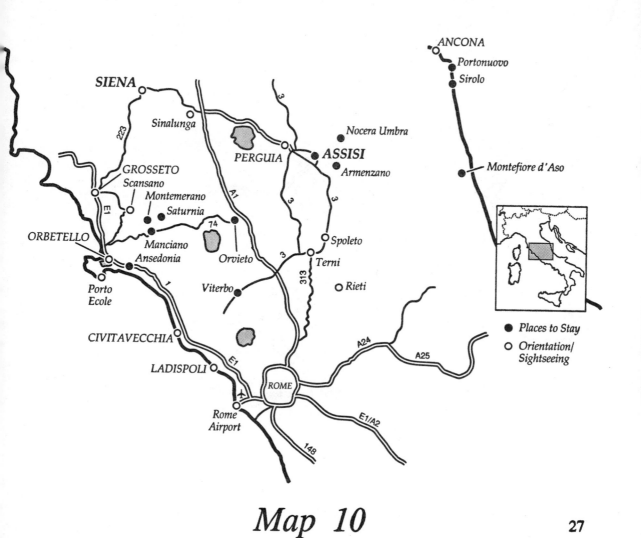

Map 10

27

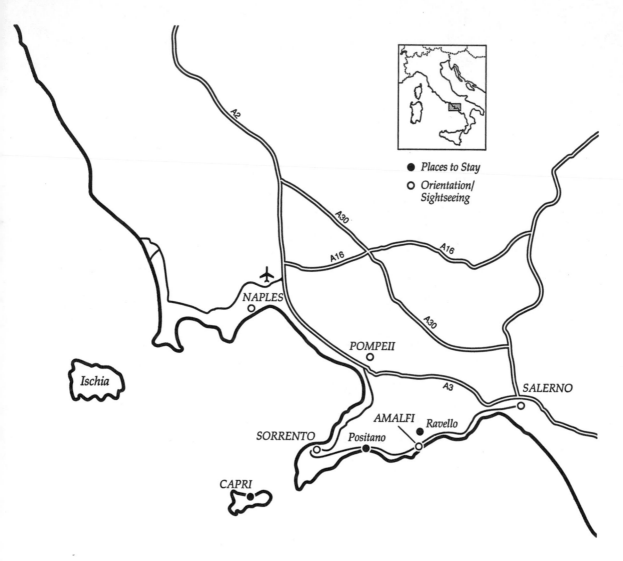

Map 11

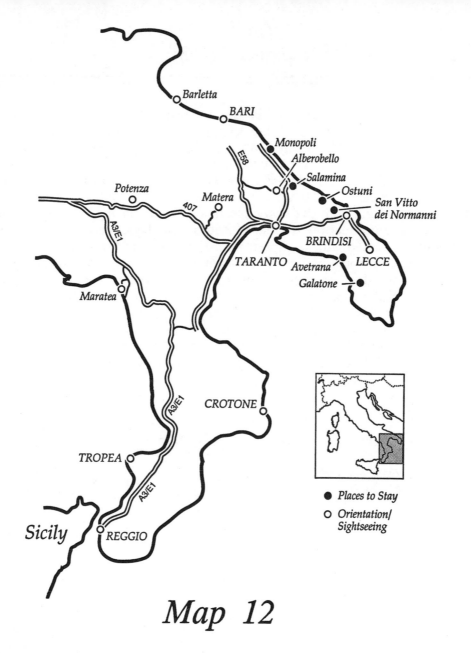

Barletta

BARI

Monopoli

E58

Alberobello

Salamina

Ostuni

Potenza

Matera

San Vitto
dei Normanni

407

A3/E1

BRINDISI

TARANTO

LECCE

Avetrana

Maratea

Galatone

A3/E1

CROTONE

TROPEA

A3/E1

Sicily

REGGIO

● Places to Stay

○ Orientation/
  Sightseeing

Map 12

In the heart of the wine valley of Piedmont, just outside and above Alba, is the stately, cream-colored villa of Giuliana Giacosa and her husband, Cascina Reine's gracious hosts.   Besides a lovely flower garden and above-ground pool, the large home has a terracotta roof, a lovely arcaded patio and a fabulous view over Alba's rooftops and the surrounding countryside.   Wicker chairs with plump floral cushions invite guests to relax on the patio, where at sunset they may also enjoy a refreshing mint drink with the *simpatico* hosts while sharing the day's adventures. At present, accommodation is offered within the ivy-covered main house, each room finely decorated with antiques, paintings and the family's personal objects. Next year, six rooms will be constructed within a storage wing adjoining the villa. Breakfast is served either outside on the patio overlooking the vineyards and orchards, or inside in the pristine dining room with vaulted ceilings.   And there's no need to worry about finding a lunch or dinner spot here, as Alba has some of the finest restaurants in Italy. The city is also famous for its wines and annual truffle festival.   *Directions:* From Alba follow signs for Altavilla and Mango.   Watch for a small sign on the left before the large wrought-iron gates.

CASCINA REINE
Host: Signori Giacosa
Altavilla 9
Alba (CN) 12051, Italy
tel: (0173) 440112
5 rooms with private bathrooms
Lire 70,000 double B&B
Breakfast only
Open all year
No English spoken
Region: Piedmont

Seven km from historic Bergamo and within easy reach of beautiful Lakes Como, Iseo and Garda is the home of the region's Agriturist president, Gianantonio Ardizzone. On Gianantonio's property, adjacent to the recently constructed residence where he lives with his wife and two sons, is a sprawling 15th-century farmhouse and barn complex of the type known in Lombard as a *cascina*. Installed within the cascina are three guest apartments, each of which includes a bedroom, living room, bathroom and kitchen. The apartments are furnished modestly but comfortably, and the ambience within and without is decidedly rustic. The cascina could perhaps use a coat of paint, but it is nestled in pretty surroundings, looking onto the small town of Nese, and backing onto the green hills where Gianantonio keeps his well-tended riding horses. No meals are served here, but a nearby trattoria adequately appeases the appetite, or you may want to do some shopping before you arrive and come prepared to prepare your own. The Grumello offers self-sufficient, conveniently located accommodation and a good value. Your hosts next door are exceptionally helpful and sincerely warm. *Directions:* Exit north from the city of Bergamo toward Nese. Turn left after a church, then right where Grumello is indicated.

CASCINA GRUMELLO
Hosts: Gianantonio Ardizzone family
Localita: Fraz. Nese
Alzano Lombardo (BG) 24022, Italy
tel: (035) 510060
3 apartments
Lire 20,000 per person
No meals served
Open all year
Some English spoken
Region: Lombard

Anna Casalini had a brilliant idea when she decided to open a small inn just outside the seaside resort of Argentario, a favorite of Romans, because she became the first in the vicinity to offer moderately priced and attractive accommodations. Only a short ride from the quaint port towns of Porto Ercole, Porto Santo Stefano, the island of Giglio, and within hailing distance of a panoramic coastal drive that rivals that of Amalfi, La Locanda guarantees a relaxing stay in an intimate setting. The inn's twelve air-conditioned guestrooms all include bathrooms, and are simply and newly appointed. Rooms off the garden are recommended as the others face the Aurelia road which can be busy. All meals are served in the public restaurant, and are taken either in the inside dining room with fireplace for the cooler months, or the glassed-in summer dining room overlooking a lush garden providing the illusion of being deep in the countryside. The cuisine is innovative and excellent, in keeping with the family's culinary tradition (they have another hotel/restaurant on the island of Giglio). *Directions:* Take the Aurelia road north from Rome. After turnoff for Ansedonia, turn right at the inn sign. From Florence take superstrada to Grosseto, then Aurelia road toward Rome, turning left after Orbetello at the inn sign.

LA LOCANDA DI ANSEDONIA
Hosts: Anna Casalini & Gabrielle Rum
Via Aurelia Sud, km 140,500
Ansedonia (GR) 58016, Italy
tel: (0564) 881317
12 rooms with private bathrooms
Lire 85,000 double B&B
All meals served
Credit cards: VS
Open all year
Very little English spoken
Region: Tuscany

Few visitors to the spiritual city of Assisi are aware that the Subasio mountains flanking it feature some of the most breathtaking scenery in the country. Nestled there is a cluster of stone houses known as Le Silve, a village which in the 10th Century served as a haven for pilgrims traveling from the Adriatic coast to Rome. In this idyllic setting they could count on a home-cooked meal and impeccable hospitality. Carrying on this tradition, Signora Taddia has recreated an ambience of utter tranquility, while adding her own touch of elegance. The guestrooms are tastefully furnished with simple antiques which blend harmoniously with the preserved medieval architecture. The main house contains sixteen bedrooms with bath and panoramic views, reception and a living room with fireplace. The auxiliary house has a beamed dining room, billiard and card rooms. This B&B features many of the amenities of a luxury hotel, including swimming pool, tennis and horseback riding. *Directions:* From Assisi go in the direction of Gualdo Tadino. One passes close to and should not miss the Eremo (site of St Francis' retreat). Take the winding uphill road at the sign for Armenzano and follow it for 15 km. The hotel is after Armenzano and is well-marked.

LE SILVE DI ARMENZANO
Host: Daniela Taddia
Localita: Armenzano
Assisi (PG) 06081, Italy
tel: (075) 8019000 fax: (075) 8019005
16 rooms with private bathrooms
Lire 200,000 double B&B
*   full- and half board available*
Credit cards: VS
Closed January and February
Fluent English spoken
Region: Umbria

Situated just a few miles from the Gulf of Taranto, and strategically based between the cities of Gallipoli, Taranto and Lecce, is the villa of Giacinto Mannarini. The sprawling, whitewashed modern inn was built on the original site of the Mudonato castle. Signor Mannarini, a retired Alitalia airline executive, offers warm hospitality in nine guestrooms with private bath on the ground floor of the main house, which are reached "motel-style" through separate entrances off an arcaded breezeway. Spotless rooms are furnished with rustic reproductions in dark wood. The property covers a 100-acres of forest and olive groves and boasts a lovely swimming pool with changing rooms and a kitchen serving meals on the poolside patio. The fine cuisine (cited in the Veronelli restaurant guide for culinary distinction) is prepared from the freshest available produce and features homemade pastas (the local *orecchiette*, or ear pasta) and desserts. Vegetarian dishes are also available. And for those tired of bread and jam, a full American breakfast is served (eggs, cheese, cereal, etc.). *Directions:* From Taranto take route 7 through Manduria and Avetrana. Five km out of town toward Salice turn left at sign for Mudonato.

CASTELLO DI MUDONATO
Host: Giacinto Mannarini
Casella Postale 2
Avetrana (TA) 74020, Italy
tel: (099) 674597
9 rooms with private bathrooms, 1 apartment
Lire 70-80,000 per person half board
   minimum stay 2 nights
Breakfast and dinner served
Closed February
English spoken well
Region: Apulia

Tucked in the hills of Montalbano, 38 km from Florence, is the lovely Bacchereto farm owned by the Bencini Tesi family, which opened its doors to guests several years ago as a sideline to its wine-production business. The farm comprises several historic buildings, the main house being where the family resides and breakfast is served. At a long table with visible signs of hundreds of years of use, guests are served fresh breads, homemade jams and honey. The best rooms are in the palazzina, an 18th-century garden villa with seven double rooms (three with private bath) tastefully furnished with family antiques. Well-worn terracotta floors and beamed ceilings add to the historic atmosphere, and the kitchen and living room are at the guests' disposal. The family owns an exceptional restaurant, La Cantina di Toia (cited in the Veronelli guide), in town within a stone building once home to Leonardo da Vinci's grandmother! Maitre d' Gennaro attends meticulously to patrons, and offers an excellent selection of wines including the estate's own chianti Carmignano of Bacchereto. *Directions:* From Florence take autostrada A1 to exit Firenze Nord/Prato. Follow signs for Poggio a Caiano, Saeno, then Bacchereto.

FATTORIA DI BACCHERETO
Hosts: Bencini Tesi family
Via Fontemorana 179
Bacchereto (FI) 50040, Italy
tel: (055) 8717191
11 rooms, 3 with private bathrooms
    4 apartments
Lire 75,000 double B&B
Trattoria on premises
Open all year
English spoken well
Region: Tuscany

Just 18 km outside the enchanting town of Lucca with its enticing shops is the lovely farmhouse of the Capparoni family. Dottore Capparoni, a renowned Roman surgeon, fondly recalls childhood vacations at his grandfather's farm and, believing visitors to the area would enjoy it, too, started offering accommodations in the main 16th-century grand villa. But he didn't stop there. Each year he added rooms in small stone houses surrounding the villa, and eventually the family property evolved into a country inn/hotel with thirty five rooms, all with private bath. Despite the "evolution," the country-home ambience has been well-preserved, and guests are made to feel at home anywhere they wander: whether in the three cozy, English-style sitting rooms, the large dining rooms, or the spectacular flower garden. A favorite treat is to unwind with a drink at sunset on the spacious terrace overlooking the hills and distant towns. Each guestroom differs in size and decor, but all are decorated with antiques and are warm and inviting. The dinner menu is planned in advance and posted each morning, giving guests ample time to make special requests should they so desire. Other activities available at the villa include swimming, billiards, ping pong and horseback riding. *Directions:* From Lucca follow signs for Ponte San Pietro, then Nozzano. Villa Casanova is well-marked just beyond Nozzano.

VILLA CASANOVA
Host: Dottor Angelo Capparoni
Balbano (LU) 55050, Italy
tel: (0583) 548429
35 rooms with private bathrooms
Lire 80,000 double B&B
Breakfast and dinner served
Open Easter-October
English spoken well
Region: Tuscany

In the heart of the Veneto region, south of Vicenza with its villas of Palladio and lush green countryside, is perched the Castello winery and estate.   The handsome 15th-century villa with its long, winding drive and arched entranceway, proudly watches over the sweet town of Barbarano Vicentino.   It has been the home of the Godi-Marinoni family for the past century.   The large walled courtyard with manicured Renaissance garden is bordered by the family's home, the guesthouse (originally farmer's quarters), and converted barn where concerts and banquets are organized.   The remaining side overlooks the family's expansive vineyards from which fine red wines are produced.   The independent guesthouse holds four bedrooms two bathrooms, a sitting room and kitchen which are divided according to the size of the group, and are decorated simply and pleasantly with the Marinoni family furnishings.   Signor Gianluigi enjoys showing guests around the property including a special visit to his wine cellar of ancient origins.   *Directions:* Exit from the A4 at Vicenza Sud towards Barbarano Vicentino.   Follow signs to Castello (20km).

IL CASTELLO
Hosts: Gianluigi and Elda Godi Marinoni
Via Castello 6
Barbarano Vicentino (VI) 36021, Italy
tel: (0444) 886055
4 rooms sharing 2 bathrooms
Lire 50,000 double
No meals served
3 day minimum stay
Open all year
English spoken well
Region: Veneto

La Casa Sola is just that: a house standing alone on a hilltop surrounded by bucolic countryside. The proprietors, a noble Genovese family, frequent their lovely vineyard property only during holidays, leaving the daily management in the capable hands of the local Regoli family. The wine- and olive-oil producing concern has also produced four large guest apartments within a rose-vine-covered stone farmhouse just down the road from the main villa. Apartment no. 3 is the loveliest. Installed on two floors comprising a living room with fireplace, kitchen, two bedrooms and two baths, the apartment is furnished in style with refined country antiques. Botanical prints hung with bows, eyelet curtains, fresh flowers and a bottle of wine are welcoming touches. The other apartments are smaller and simpler, but each opens onto a private garden. An inviting cypress-edged swimming pool overlooking the valley has recently been added. The Casa Sola requires a minimum week's stay, and provides an ideal touring base in a tranquil, romantic setting for more independent travelers. *Directions:* Exit at San Donato off the Firenze-Siena superstrada. After San Donato, turn right onto dirt road at sign for Cortine/Casa Sola, and follow for 7 km.

FATTORIA CASA SOLA
Hosts: Count Gambaro family
Localita: Cortine
Barberino Val d'Elsa (FI) 50021, Italy
tel. & fax: (055) 8075028
4 apartments
Lire 650,000-1,200,000 weekly according
  to apartment size and season
Occasional dinner served upon request
Open all year
Little English spoken
Region: Tuscany

Just off the main road midway between Siena and Florence, the highlight cities of Tuscany, is the square stone farmhouse with cupola owned and operated by Gianni and Cristina, a young couple from Milan.   The Paretaio is particularly appealing to visitors with a passion for horseback riding, for the energetic proprietors offer everything from basic riding lessons to dressage training to day outings through the gorgeous surrounding countryside. With that agenda, plus 20 horses to choose from, the Paretaio is recognized as one of the top riding "ranches" in Tuscany. Next to the saddle room on the first floor is a rustic and warm living room with country antiques and comfy sofas, enhanced by a vaulted brick ceiling and worn terracotta floors.   Upstairs, the main gathering area is the dining room which features a massive fireplace and a seemingly endless wooden table.   For lunch and dinner, each guest pulls up a chair to share the table and a savory Tuscan meal. Access to the seven bedrooms is from this room, and each is stylishly decorated with touches such as dried flowers, white lace curtains and, not surprisingly, equestrian prints.   Although riding is the main activity here, the Paretaio is an excellent base for touring the heart of Tuscany.   *Directions:* Heading south from Barberino, the Paretaio is just off the road at the second right-hand turnoff.

IL PARETAIO
Hosts: Cristina & Gianni De Marchi
Localita: San Filippo
Barberino Val D'Elsa (FI) 50021, Italy
tel: (055) 8075324
7 rooms, 2 with private bathrooms
Lire 75-90,000 per person full board (required)
Open Easter-November
English spoken well
Region: Tuscany

Conveniently located between Siena and Florence in the heart of Chianti, while affording a feeling of escape from the rest of the world, is the La Chiara farm, dating back to 1600.   Covering 45-hectares of woods, vineyards and olive groves, the busy establishment is run by several families who came to this haven from Milan and reside in the stone houses surrounding the main villa.   Twelve bedrooms, five of which have private baths, are dispersed throughout the informal household, which also contains a large living room, kitchen, and dining room where mostly farm-fresh vegetarian meals are served.   The common rooms and the high-ceilinged bedrooms are very modestly furnished with worn country furniture, but are spacious and airy, offering scenic views over the serene countryside.   Extra beds can be easily added to rooms, making the Chiara an ideal choice for families traveling with small children.   Headed by young and extremely personable Gaia and her husband, the farm swarms with activity when groups come for special lectures and courses on art and psychology.   A small swimming pool not far from the house is open to guests.   *Directions:* From Barberino take the road towards Cortine.   At the fork, bear right and continue 7 km to the Chiara farm.

LA CHIARA
Hosts: Gaia Mezzadri & families
Localita: Prumiano
Barberino Val d'Elsa (FI) 50021, Italy
tel: (055) 8075330
12 rooms, 5 with private bathrooms
Lire 70,000 double
Breakfast and dinner served
Open March-December
English spoken well
Region: Tuscany

On the list of bed and breakfasts with unique locations is the Dreikirchen, situated up in the Dolomite foothills with an enchanting view over a lush green valley and distant snowcapped mountain peaks. The young and energetic Wodenegg family works diligently at running the summer-season inn and restaurant and at making guests feel at home in their lovely residence. Their restaurant receives non-guest patrons as well since it shares the site of a unique historical monument: *Le Tre Chiese,* three curious, attached miniature churches which date back to the Middle Ages. The inn is reachable by either calling to be met by jeep, or on foot. An exhilarating half-hour hike takes you up to the typical mountain-style chalet with front wooden balconies. A new addition has been recently constructed, but the most charming rooms are those in the older section, entirely wood-paneled, with fluffy comforters and old-fashioned wash basins. The rambling house has several common areas for guests as well as a swimming pool and tennis courts. Truly an incredible spot, near Siusi and Val Gardena. *Directions:* Exit from the Bolzano-Brennero autostrada at Klausen and take the road to and through Barbian to Bad Dreikirchen's parking on the right. Call the hotel from the bar across the street and they will send a jeep to collect you.

BAD DREIKIRCHEN
Hosts: The Wodenegg family
Localita: Tre Chiese
Barbian, (BZ) 39040, Italy
tel: (0471) 654155
35 rooms sharing bathrooms
Lire 60,000 per person half board
All meals served
Open Easter-September
Some English spoken
Region: Trentino Alto Adige

The Locanda, a pale-yellow and brick villa dating from 1830, sits on the border between Tuscany and Umbria and serves as an excellent base from which to explore this rich countryside.   The villa's dining room features a vaulted ceiling in toast-colored brick, an enormous fireplace, French windows opening out to the flower garden, and antiques including a cupboard adorned with the family's blue-and-white china.   The upstairs quarters are reserved primarily for guests, and contain six comfortable rooms which share four baths and an inviting sitting room and library.   The cozy bedrooms have mansard ceilings, armoires, lovely linens and wash basins.   A suite and an additional guestroom are located on the ground floor in the opposite wing, once used for drying tobacco.   These accommodations, each with private bath, are decorated with antique reproductions and appear more modern.   The young hostess, Palmira, besides being a wonderful cook, enjoys planning daily excursions with her guests.   Siena is only 55 km away, and the quaint medieval and renaissance villages of Pienza, Montepulciano and Montalcino are close by.   *Directions:* Exit from the Rome-Florence autostrada at Valdichiana. Head toward Bettolle, then bear right toward Siena.   Follow signs for Bandita.

LOCANDA LA BANDITA
Host: Palmira Fiorini
Via Bandita 72
Bettolle (SI) 53040, Italy
tel: (0577) 624649
8 rooms, 2 with private bathrooms
Lire 70,000 per person half board
*   (with private bath)*
Breakfast and dinner served
Open all year
English spoken well
Region: Tuscany

This guide includes some small bed-and-breakfast-like urban hotels for the convenience of travelers who would like to do some metropolitan sightseeing. For some reason, the city of Bologna is often bypassed by visitors, despite its rich past, beautiful historic center, arcaded streets and elegant shops. Mentioned in another of these guides, *Italian Country Inns & Itineraries,* is the splendid Hotel Corona d'Oro, whose owner, Signor Mauro Orsi, owns two other centrally located, smaller hotels: the Orologio and the Commercianti. Steps away from Bologna's main piazza and Basilica is the recently renovated Orologio, so-called because it looks onto city hall with its clock tower. The hotel has twenty five rooms on three floors, and the intimate atmosphere of a family-run establishment. The newly remodeled guestrooms are pleasantly decorated with pretty floral-print wallpaper, photographs of the city from the 1930s and simple reproduction furniture. An unusual but welcome treat is the full breakfast buffet served in the dining room. Signor Orsi's other "urban inn," the modern Commercianti, is scheduled for remodeling in the near future, when an effort will be made to have the decor more closely reflect the building's 13th-century vintage.

HOTEL OROLOGIO
Host: Mauro Orsi
Via IV Novembre 10
Bologna 40123, Italy
tel: (051) 231253 fax: (051) 260552
25 rooms with private bathrooms
Lire 150,000 double B&B
Breakfast only
Credit cards: AX VS
Open all year
English spoken well
Region: Emilia-Romagna

Brisighella is a gem. The town comes to life during June and July when it celebrates its annual Medieval Festival. Medieval games are re-enacted, and period music, literature and dance are produced. Locals attire themselves in appropriate costume and the village's narrow streets are illuminated nightly by torches for the occasion. Just out of town past the thermal hot springs is the sweet home of a young Milanese couple, Ettore and Barbara, who moved here recently, taking over the vineyards and orchards of the 10- hectare property. They have renovated the barn next to their small stone house, creating three guestrooms as well as a rustic dining area with exposed beams and a large fireplace where guests gather for meals. Each room, decorated with simple country furnishings, has its own bathroom. The atmosphere is casual and the value excellent. While in the vicinity don't miss the mosaics in Ravenna, the historical center of Bologna and the international ceramic museum in Faenza. *Directions:* Take Faenza exit from the A14 between Bologna and Rimini. Follow signs for Brisighella. At town take left turn for Terme/Modigliona. Il Palazzo is the third house on the left.

IL PALAZZO
Hosts: Ettore Matarese family
Via Baccagnano 11
Brisighella (RA) 40013, Italy
tel: (0546) 80338
3 rooms with private bathrooms
Lire 50,000 double B&B
Breakfast and dinner served
Open all year
English spoken well
Region: Emilia-Romagna

For those who have a passion for horseback riding, or with an urge to learn, La Mandria provides the opportunity to do either while on holiday. As host and horseman Davide Felice Aondio proudly explains, his horse farm has been in existence for over 30 years and was the model for riding resorts. Situated near the foothills of the Alps and between the cities of Turin and Milan, the vast, flat property borders a 5,000-hectare state park, offering spectacular scenery and endless possibilities for horseback excursions. The complex is made up of horse stables, haylofts, guestrooms, dining room and the private homes of the proprietor and his son's family. The whole forms a square with riding rings in the center. As a national equestrian training center, lessons of every nature are offered for all ages. Six very basic bedrooms with bath are reserved for guests, and good local fare is served in the rustic dining room. Golf, swimming and tennis facilities are available nearby. Two sidetrips that must not be missed are to spellbinding Lake Maggiore, and to the intriguing medieval town of Ricetto where the houses and streets are made of smooth stones. *Directions:* Take Carisio exit from the Milan-Turin autostrada. Head toward Biella, but at town of Candelo turn right for Mottalciata. Mandria is on the right.

LA MANDRIA
Hosts: Aondio family
Candelo (VC) 13062, Italy
tel: (015) 53078
6 rooms with private bathrooms
Lire 130,000 per person full board
  with horseback riding
Open all year
English spoken well
Region: Piedmont

Poetically named after a classic Italian tale by Cesare Pavese, a native of this area, the Luna e I Falo (meaning the moon and the fire) farmhouse was lovingly restored by Turin couple Ester and Franco Carnero. The ritual described in the story is still performed on the eighth of August every year when local farmers collect old grapevines and burn them under the full moon in hopes of a good crop. On that night, the bonfires dotting hills surrounding the farm create quite a spectacle. The Carnero's brick home has arched windows and an arcaded front terrace, and the two double rooms and one suite they have made available to visitors are within. For a country home, the spacious living/dining area is elaborately furnished with Renaissance period pieces. The bedrooms reveal a combination of old and new decor and sweeping views of the countryside, known for its wineries. The emphasis at the Luna e I Falo is on the cuisine, and logically so. The proprietors previously owned a highly regarded restaurant in Turin, and they did not leave their culinary skills behind. They continue to practice them, producing excellent handmade pasta (no machines in Ester's kitchen!), among other delicacies. *Directions:* From Asti follow the signs for Canelli and, before town, take a right up the hill to Castello. The farmhouse is on the right side.

LA LUNA E I FALO
Hosts: Ester & Franco Carnero
Localita Aie 37
Canelli (AT) 14053, Italy
tel: (0141) 831643
3 rooms with private bathrooms
Lire 70,000 double B&B
Dinner served upon request
Open all year
No English spoken (French)
Region: Piedmont

North of Florence between Prato and Pistoia is a pocket of little-known, yet entrancing countryside comprising the Calvana Mountains and Bisenzio Valley. Grazia, Mario and their three children have lived there all their lives and love sharing their enthusiasm for the area through offering accommodation to visitors. Although the entrance and exterior leave a little to be desired in terms of aesthetics, the property is beautifully situated overlooking a wooded valley and private lake out the back. What really counts here is the hosts' warmth and their sincere effort to make their guests feel at home. The six bedrooms with accompanying immaculate baths are sweet and simple, decorated with comfortable, old-fashioned furniture. Guests convene downstairs for breakfast and dinner in the rustic dining room with exposed beams and fireplace, off of which is the kitchen, where you can watch Grazia rolling out fresh pasta. From lasagna and tortelli to polenta and desserts, Grazia's culinary arts reflect the influence of the bordering regions of Tuscany and Emilia. A visit to the welcoming Ponte alla Villa offers an opportunity to familiarize yourself with the customs of a part of the country that is off the beaten track. *Directions:* From Prato, take route 325 north to Vernio, then bear left toward Cantagallo. Watch for signs for the B&B at Luicciana.

PONTE ALLA VILLA
Hosts: Grazia Gori & Mario Michelagnoli
Localita Luicciana
La Villa 273
Cantagallo (FI) 50040, Italy
tel: (0574) 956094
6 rooms with private bathrooms
Lire 38,000 per person half board
Breakfast and dinner served
Open all year
Very little English spoken
Region: Tuscany

The Via Tragara is undoubtedly the most beautiful street in Capri. It is lined with stately villas overlooking the sea and surrounded by lush vegetation. Halfway along it on the left is the Certosella, which means little convent in Italian, the hotel's origin over 300 years ago. This enchanting property is entered through a romantic overgrown arbored garden lined with hundreds of flower pots. An eclectically decorated entrance/living room welcomes guests downstairs, while upstairs are located four bedrooms, each with its own bath and personality. With their massive wood doors, high ceilings and heavy antiques, they give the impression of being untouched for the past century or so. There is an appealing sense of clutter and lack of tidy perfection about the place which will probably disappear entirely as the building is remodeled over the next few years. In fact, the work has begun; a new wing has been added with six more bedrooms, a restaurant and a swimming pool. These more luxurious accommodations will be available sometime this year at different rates. At the very end of the Tragara, down many hundreds of steps and in front of the Faraglioni rocks, you'll find owner Luigi's restaurant, called Luigi ai Faraglioni, and a bathing area. *Directions:* Take cable car up to Capri, walk through the square, then down Via Emanuele to Via Tragara.

LA CERTOSELLA
Host: Luigi Jacono
Via Tragara 13-15
Capri (NA) 80073, Italy
tel: (081) 8370713
10 rooms with private bathrooms
Lire 140,000 double B&B
Breakfast and dinner served
Open Easter-October
Some English spoken
Region: Campania

La Minerva is located in a quiet section of Capri, slightly off the beaten track, yet still quite central, permitting easy access to the more bustling areas of town, a walker's paradise with no motorized transportation allowed. The street-level entrance is the hotel's third-floor living room, a vast chamber with stark-white tiled floors and ground-to-ceiling windows overlooking the sea. This captivating view will strike you every time you come or go or eat breakfast, as the same panorama greets you in the dining room. The rest of the small hotel is beneath, with the reception and breakfast area on the ground floor. Signora Esposito has decorated the eighteen rooms sweetly and simply with colorful tiled floors and scattered antiques. Each bedroom has a private balcony overlooking umbrella-pine woods and the sea. All rooms also have their own bath, done in blue and white tile. The family lives in one section of the building, but share with guests their homey living room, with family photos and lace doilies on the tables. This is a peaceful spot to get away, but not too far away. *Directions:* It's best to stop by the tourist office as you get off the ferry and get a map of Capri, showing the Via Occhio Marino.

LA MINERVA
Hosts: Esposito family
Via Occhio Marino 8
Capri (NA) 80073, Italy
tel: (081) 8377067/8375201
18 rooms with private bathrooms
Lire 140,000 double B&B
*   160,000 high season*
Breakfast only
Credit cards: all major
Open Easter-October
Some English spoken
Region: Campania

The Villa Krupp is a delightful small hotel whose claim to local fame can be found in its guestbook, boasting such illustrious names as Lenin and Gorky. Signor Coppola, the cordial and proud proprietor, took over the property in 1964. The charming hotel contains twelve bedrooms, each with its own bath, in a somewhat modern and boxy building alongside the host's own residence. The Krupp is dramatically situated in one of the most beautiful corners of Capri's Augusto Park, atop a steep, sheer cliff dropping to the sparkling turquoise sea beneath. The site overlooks the Faraglioni rock formation (a symbol of the island) and Marina Piccola, one of Capri's two ports. A thousand steps lead from its top edge down to the seaside. The Villa Krupp has its own set of steps leading up to the best vantage point from which to admire this spectacular panorama. The light-filled guestrooms each feature their own terrace and bath, are decorated with simple antiques and tiled with the brightly colored ceramics typical of Capri. Room #18 is a particular favorite due to its relatively large seaview terrace. Breakfast is served in the veranda or outside on the flowered terrace. *Directions:* Take the cable car up to Capri, walk through the main square, then down the Via Emanuele to Matteotti (on the right).

VILLA KRUPP
Hosts: The Coppola family
Viale Matteotti 12
Capri (NA) 80073, Italy
tel: (081) 8370362
12 rooms with private bathrooms
Lire 135,000 double B&B
Breakfast only
Open all year
Some English spoken
Region: Campania

Capri has long had a reputation for being an exclusive island. Charging prices substantially higher than the rest of the country, only the elite were able to afford to vacation there. However, times have changed and the cost of tourism across Italy has soared, bringing other destinations more in line with Capri in terms of expense, therefore making it relatively more affordable than it once was. Unfortunately, agritourism does not exist on the island, but there are several small, family-run hotels that provide a bed and breakfast "feeling." One such establishment belongs to Antonino Vuotto and his wife, a local couple who have opened up their centrally located prim white home in the town of Capri, making four bedrooms available to guests. The rooms are very clean and neat, with typically tiled floors, and private baths and balconies in each. Breakfast is brought to your room (there is no common dining room), and is the only meal served, but the Villa's convenient location makes it easy to get to one of Capri's fine restaurants for lunch and dinner. *Directions:* Take the cable car up to Capri. Go through the main town square to Via Emanuele, past the Quisisana Hotel and continue to the end of the street. Turn left onto Via Certosa, then left again on Cerio. The Villa is on the corner and is not marked with a sign.

VILLA VUOTTO
Hosts: Antonino Vuotto family
Via Campo di Teste 2
Capri (NA) 80073, Italy
tel: (081) 8370230
4 rooms with private bathrooms
Lire 100,000 double B&B
Breakfast only
Open all year
No English spoken
Region: Campania

The Ombria farmhouse nestles amidst the foothills just 30 km from both beautifully austere Bergamo and Lecco at Lake Como. Meticulous restoration of the stone house dating from 1613 began over two years ago and should be completed this spring. Although not yet open when we visited, the attention to detail and authenticity evident so far (such as the faithful reproduction of the original stone floor patterns), along with host Luciano's description, contain great promise. An arched entryway leads into a stone courtyard with gazebo and open grill, where tables will be set for summertime meals. The Ombria has already made a name for itself with its exceptional restaurant where patrons enjoy candlelit international cuisine in the intimate stone-walled dining room--as long as they make reservations three months in advance! Luciano retired early to realize his dream of running a country inn and breeding French and Swiss goats for cheese. The four doubles and two suites available are to be decorated with fine antiques and wrought-iron beds. Original fireplaces, exposed beams, warm wood floors, stone walls and a common cozy sitting room should make them particularly appealing. A pool is planned for the end of 1992. *Directions:* Take the A4 autostrada from Milan, exit at Agrate and head north toward Lecco on Route 36. At route 342 turn right toward Caprino Bergamasco and follow signs for Ombria.

OMBRIA
Host: Luciano Marchesin
Localita: Celana
Caprino Bergamasco (BG) 24030, Italy
tel: (035) 781668
4 rooms and 2 suites with private bathrooms
Lire 35,000 per person half board
All meals served
Open Easter-October
English spoken well
Region: Lombardy

West of Chianti, just behind the medieval hilltop village of Casole d'Elsa, and half an hour from the picturesque towns of Siena and San Gimignano, is a typical Tuscan stone farmhouse. It is this place that the eight-member Zito family has called home for the past six years, ever since they made the unanimous and courageous decision to uproot from New York and start over in Italy, blending almost seamlessly into the culture and tranquil lifestyle of their country of origin. Together they took on the project of restoring the house, landscaping, and furnishing the seven guestrooms on the second floor above their living quarters. The bedrooms, each with spotless blue-and-white-tiled bathrooms and welcoming flowers, retain a simple country flavor, enhanced by the worn terracotta brick floors, beamed ceilings, antique armoires and bedside tables, and wrought-iron beds. A large living area with fireplace and kitchenette is reserved for guests. Breakfast consisting of fresh-baked cakes and breads is served until noon outside on the rose-covered stone patio overlooking the hillsides and herds of sheep. Judging by the appreciative comments in the guest book, it is evident that Alfred and Rose have offered much happiness to many travelers. *Directions:* From Florence take the superstrada toward Siena, exiting at Colle Val d'Elsa. Take Route 68 and turn left for Casole d'Elsa. The inn is just outside town beyond the Hotel Pietralta.

PODERE CAPRETTO
Hosts: Alfred & Rose Zito
Casole d'Elsa (SI) 53031, Italy
tel: (0577) 948550
7 rooms with private bathrooms
Lire 80,000 double B&B
Breakfast only
Open all year
Fluent English spoken
Region: Tuscany

What a pleasant surprise to discover the Solarola, a sunny yellow villa as its name implies, in the flat Midwest-like countryside around Bologna. It is, in a word, perfect. Gracious hosts Antonella and Valentino (a renowned architect), took over the family farm several years ago, transforming one of its two turn-of-the-century villas into a private home and the other into a guest house with three double rooms and one suite, as well as a restaurant, living room, billiard room and outdoor gazebo. Antonella decorated the guest villa to be romantic and refined, yet warm and inviting, without a single detail overlooked. Each room is named after a flower and everything from wallpaper, botanical prints and fluffy comforters to motifs on lamp shades and bed frames, bouquets and even room fragrance conform to the floral theme in color and appearance. The hosts' passion for the Victorian period is apparent in details such as cupboards filled with china, lace curtains and doilies, dried-flower bouquets, old family photos and Tiffany lamps. In addition, Antonella has been praised in several publications for her refined cuisine, creating inventive combinations with the freshest of ingredients to the delight of guests. A first-rate splurge. *Directions:* Best to call from town, as there are few signs.

LOCANDA SOLAROLA
Hosts: Antonella Scardovi & Valentino Parmiani
Via San Croce 5
Castel Guelfo (BO) 40023, Italy
tel: (0542) 53951
3 doubles and 1 suite with private bathrooms
Lire 240,000 double B&B
Breakfast and dinner served
Credit cards: VS AX
Closed August
English spoken well
Region: Emilia-Romagna

The Villa Gaidello farm has been written up on several occasions (in *Bon Appetit, Cuisine, Eating in Italy*), mostly as a result of its superb cuisine. There is nothing extravagant about hostess Paola Bini's recipes, carefully prepared by local women. Rather, the secret to her success seems to lie in the revival of basic traditional dishes using the freshest possible ingredients. Pasta is made daily (a great treat to watch) and features all the local variations on tagliatelle, pappardelle and stricchettoni. Reservations for dinner must be made several days in advance. Paola was one of the pioneers in agriturismo, transforming her grandmother's nearly 200-year-old farmhouse into a guest house and restaurant 20 years ago. One to five guests are accommodated in each of the three suites, which include kitchen and sitting room. The suites are cozy and rustic with exposed-brick walls, country antiques and lace curtains. The dining room, set with doilies and ceramic, is situated in the converted hayloft and overlooks the garden and a small pond. The Gaidello provides a convenient stopover just off the Bologna-Milan autostrada. *Directions*: Exit the autostrada at Castelfranco, Modena Sud. Follow Via Emilia/Route 9, turning left at the sign for Gaidello.

VILLA GAIDELLO
Host: Paola Bini
Via Gaidello 22
Castelfranco Emilia (MO) 41013, Italy
tel: (059) 926806
3 suites with private bathrooms
Lire 138,000 double B&B
Breakfast and dinner served
Open all year
English spoken very well
Region: Emilia-Romagna

The Podere San Quirico is a sweet little Tuscan farmhouse with an even sweeter owner and hostess, Maria Consiglio Picone, a former theater costume designer who moved to Tuscany from her native Naples 22 years ago. Her B&B activity commenced soon afterward, once the 14th-century crumbling stone farmhouse had been lovingly pieced back together. Maria proudly points out how the original exposed-beam structure dating from 1300 has been kept intact, and how her enchanting garden has developed over the years. Four guestrooms within her home are decorated in harmony with the house, containing simple country furniture and wrought-iron beds. Each room has its own spotless bath, as well as a gorgeous view over the soft green countryside. The former horse stalls have been converted into a dining room and kitchen for convenience of visitors. For weekly stays, a separate two-bedroom house is also available. Just half an hour from Siena (a must-see destination in this vicinity), and at the foot of the Chianti region, the San Quirico serves as an ideal touring base. *Directions:* Depending on the direction of your approach, exit either at Monte San Savino or Valdarno off the A1 Firenze-Roma highway. Follow signs for Castelnuovo Berardenga. The B&B is just outside town and well-marked.

PODERE SAN QUIRICO
Host: Maria Consiglio Picone
Via del Paradiso 3
Castelnuovo Berardenga (SI) 53019, Italy
tel: (0577) 355206
4 rooms with private bathrooms
1 house
Lire 88,000 double
Breakfast served on request
Open all year
English spoken well
Region: Tuscany

To the west of Cortina, the most fashionable ski area in the Dolomites, is Val Gardena, almost too storybook perfect to be true. The valley, once part of Austria, still preserves its Germanic heritage, evident in the language, cuisine and culture. It has always been a favorite vacation spot for Italians, offering good value not only in the winter, but during the hot month of August, when visitors can take hikes in the cool woods and sleep well at night under a comforter. The Gshtroffhof, owned by the warm-hearted Rier family, is right in the heart of the valley on the road leading up to the Alps of Siusi. Dating back to 1500, it is a typical white chalet with wood trim and shutters, whose 's windowsills and balconies overflow with cascading geraniums of all colors. The four guestrooms are simple and cozy, as is the rest of the house, and share nearby bathrooms. Decorated modestly with light pinewood furniture, each has a balcony affording splendid views over the green valley, snowcapped peaks and the quaint town of Siusi below. As with most farm families here, the Rier's main livelihood is raising cows, whose bells produce the only sound breaking the tranquility of the valley. *Directions:* From the Verona-Brennero autostrada, take exit Bolzano Nord and follow signs for Siusi. After town, turn right for Alps, then left at the sign for Gschtroffhof.

GSCHTROFFHOF
Hosts: Hermann Rier family
San Valentino 36
Castelrotto (BZ) 39040, Italy
tel: (0471) 706525
4 rooms sharing bathrooms
Lire 40,000 double B&B
Breakfast only
Open all year
No English spoken (German)
Region: Alto Adige

Rier is a common family name in the Val Gardena area and, though neighbors, the Rier family which owns the Marmsolerhof bears no relation to the proprietors of the Gschtrtoffhof. This adorable bed and breakfast is owned and run by a young local couple with four children. The crisp white house with its old stone-and-wood attached barn has been in the same family for over 400 years and has been recently renovated, giving the property a fresh new look. The entrance foyer walls are adorned with antique farm tools, harnesses and cow bells. On the same floor is a dining room with individual tables where guests can enjoy breakfast with a view out over the velvet green hillside. The five guestrooms, all but one with private bath, are simply and comfortably furnished with pinewood beds and armoires, bright-orange curtains and fluffy comforters. Stepping out on the balcony reveals a breathtaking panorama of the pine-covered mountains. The Riers are happy to suggest scenic places to explore by car or on foot, and know the best places for rock climbing up into one of the most spectacular ranges in Europe. *Directions:* Exit at Bolzano Nord from the Verona-Brennero autostrada and follow signs for Siusi. Beyond town, before Castelrotto, turn right for Alps, then left for Marmsolerhof.

MARMSOLERHOF
Hosts: August Rier family
San Valentino 35
Castelrotto (BZ) 39040, Italy
tel: (0471) 71514
5 rooms, 4 with private bathrooms
Lire 50,000 double B&B
Breakfast only
Open all year
Very little English spoken (German)
Region: Alto Adige

Tucked away off a winding mountain road in the enchanting Siusi Alps is a typical Tyrolian farmhouse, called *mas* in this northern region of Alto Adige.   The Jaider family has resided here ever since the 15th Century, traditionally maintaining a dairy farm.   Their inviting home is colorfully accented with green shutters and laden flower boxes at every window.   Two wooden barns are connected to the residence via a stone terrace.   Signora Jaider runs her home with the hotel efficiency which has come to expected by visitors to this predominantly German-speaking area, once belonging to Austria.   Meals are served out on the terrace in clement weather, or in the original dining room, whose charm is enhanced by the low, wood-paneled ceiling (so constructed to retain heat) with its handpainted edelweiss flowers.   Cuisine in this region reflects its Austrian heritage, with speck ham, meat and potatoes, and apple strudels winning over pasta dishes.   Lovely country antiques are dispersed around the house and throughout the eight bedrooms, which are wood-paneled from floor to ceiling and have pretty valley views.   Two guestrooms include balconies.   *Directions:* Exit at Bolzano Nord from autostrada A22, following signs for Fie and Alpe di Siusi.   Pass through Siusi and turn off to the left for Tisana.   San Osvaldo is on the left after Tisana.

TSCHOTSCHERHOF
Hosts: Jaider family
San Osvaldo 19
Castelrotto (BZ) 39040, Italy
tel: (0471) 706013
8 rooms with private bathrooms
Lire 50,000 double B&B
All meals served
Open March-October and Christmas
Very little English spoken (German)
Region: Alto Adige

Liguria is the sliver of a region touching France and boasting the Italian Riviera, including such celebrated port towns as Portofino, Santa Margherita, San Remo and Cinque Terre. Agriturismo is something new for the Ligurians; tourism has always drifted seaward. From the busy coastal town of Sestri Levante, a 6 km winding road leads up a mountain to the Monte Pu farm, where a group of people from Milan migrated in search of a simpler and saner way of life. For serenity, they could hardly have chosen a more ideal or isolated spot. The three-story, peach-color brick farmhouse complex, dating from 1400, commands a marvelous sweeping view over wooded mountains and valleys down to the sea 700 feet below. The six guestrooms (with three baths close by), are simple and immaculate, with light pine furniture and wildflower bouquets. Downstairs is the warm and airy dining room where a full country breakfast awaits guests each morning. Dinner is prepared by either Cristina or Fabrizio and served outside in the courtyard in warmer months. The culinary emphasis is on vegetarian dishes such as risotto, soups and salads, prepared with ingredients straight from the garden. Horses are available for riding in the forest preserves surrounding the property. *Directions:* Exit from the Genova-Livorno autostrada at Sestre Levante and follow signs for Cazaro Liguria, Castiglione, and then Campegli to Monte Pu.

MONTE PU
Host: Aurora Giani
Castiglione Chiavarese (GE) 16030, Italy
tel: (0185) 408.027
6 rooms sharing 3 bathrooms
Lire 80,000 double B&B
All meals served
Open Easter-November
Some English spoken
Region: Liguria

On a hilltop in Pomino wine country sits the 15th-century Medici villa that belongs to the Nicolodi family, only the third proprietors. Surrounded by hundreds of acres of scenic vineyards, olive groves and cypress woods, the large ivy-covered villa also features a renaissance garden with stone statues. Within the historic villa are six comfortable guestrooms, three with private bath. The home is steeped in the past, and the decor and knick-knacks throughout make for a visual treat. With its elaborate, worn antiques, gilt mirrors, period paintings, oriental carpets, chandeliers, and enormous gray-stone fireplaces, the place seems frozen in time. Yet a casual and welcoming atmosphere is sensed immediately. And this is how the Nicolodis like it. They put on no false airs and guests may wander about freely. Their home is literally your home. Signora is Neopolitan, as her cooking confirms, and Signor, who has traveled widely and spent a long period in Africa, sincerely enjoy receiving guests at home. And with facilities for tennis, swimming, and billiards, a jacuzzi, beautiful scenery and excellent meals (including full American-style breakfast), they do a good job of keeping them there. *Directions:* From Florence follow signs for Pontassieve. After Rufina, turn right for Pomina.

LA SOSTA AI BUSINI
Hosts: Marcello Nicolodi family
Localita Castiglioni di Rufina
Via Scopeti 77
Rufina (FI) 50068, Italy
tel: (055) 8397809   fax: (055) 8397004
6 rooms, 3 with private bathrooms
Lire 100,000 per person half board
Breakfast and dinner served
Open Easter-October
Some English spoken
Region: Tuscany

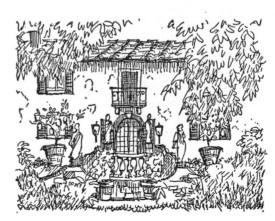

The Pomurlo farm is home to the congenial Minghelli family and covers 370-acres of hills, woods and open fields. Its location provides an excellent base from which to tour the marvels of Umbria. A winding dirt road leads past the horse stables and riding rings to the typical stone house which contains the restaurant. Inside, the tables are covered with crisp white linen, and an antique cupboard and old farm implements on the walls enhance the rustic setting. An enticing menu featuring farm-fresh specialties tempts visitors to linger over a hearty meal. Three "country suites" are situated beneath the restaurant, each consisting of two bedrooms, bathroom and kitchenette. Comfortable and cheerful, the suites are decorated with wrought-iron beds, colorful bedspreads and typical regional country antiques. A nearby converted stall houses two adorable independent rooms looking out over the lake. Other guest rooms are found in two large hilltop homes commanding a breathtaking view of the entire valley, with its grazing herds of long-horn cattle. The main house, a 12th-century tower fortress where the inn's personable hostess Daniela resides, accommodates guests in three additional suites of rooms. *Directions:* Take the Orvieto exit off of the A1 autostrada. Follow signs for Todi. On route N448 turn right at sign for Pomurlo.

POMURLO VECCHIO
Hosts: Lazzaro Minghelli & family
Localita: Lago di Corbara
Baschi (TR) 05023, Italy
tel: (0744) 950190/950475
14 rooms and suites, most with private bathrooms
Lire 68,000 per person half board
Trattoria on premises
Open all year
Some English spoken
Region: Umbria

La Mongolfiera is one of the handful of luxurious B&Bs included in this guide. Located in the Franciacorta wine region just south of Lake Iseo between the major cities of Bergamo and Brescia, this ivy-covered guest house is part of the vast Bellavista wine estate owned by Signor Vittorio Moretti. Perched idyllically on a hilltop overlooking a valley carpeted with grape vines, the small inn has six elegant bedrooms with private bath, telephone, TV and minibar. Original decorations such as colorful ceramic tile interspersed in the terracotta floors, handpainted nature motifs (birds, butterflies, fruit, flowers), and tapestry bedspreads coordinate perfectly with the fine antique furniture. Four rooms have their own terrace, and the "Sunflower" room is a suite with an extra bed in the loft. Guests have full access to the house, whose spacious downstairs includes a living room, a splendid country-style dining room with fruit garlands painted between the windows, a card room with grand piano, and an outdoor patio filled with overflowing flowerpots where dinner is served, weather permitting. *Directions:* Take the Rovato exit from the Milan-Venice A4 highway. Head toward Erbusco, turning right at the main square in town, then follow signs to Mongolfiera/Bellavista.

LA MONGOLFIERA
Host: Vittorio Moretti
Localita: Bellavista
Erbusco (BS) 25030, Italy
tel: (030) 7268451 fax: (030) 7268466
6 rooms with private bathrooms
Lire 190,000 double B&B (3-day minimum)
  137,000 per person half board
All meals served
Open all year
English spoken well
Region: Lombardia

For travelers who want to explore another facet of Italy's many-sided culture, the southern-most, "heel-side" tip of the boot-shaped peninsula, known as Puglia, merits investigation.   It is a land with spectacular coastlines, villages with distinct Greek and Turkish influence, endless lines of olive groves, fields of wild flowers, and a rich history of art including Pugliese Romanesque and Baroque (Bari's Santa Nicola church is simply one of the most beautiful in Italy).   All of this plus exquisite cuisine and a warm and open population await in Puglia, as does the Masseria Salamina, a 16th-century fortified farmhouse located between Bari and Brindisi.   The driveway leads us to the sand-colored castle with turreted tower with expansive vistas sweeping to the sea.   The farm covers hundreds of acres of land and produces primarily olive oil.   Through the courtyard are found the eight suites, each with a separate entrance and freshly decorated with reproductions and wicker furniture.   Host Gianvincenzo and family live in the main wing and run their masseria with hotel efficiency and service.   A large lofty restaurant with terracotta floors provides all meals for guests.   By this spring seven additional apartments should be available for longer stays.   *Directions:* From the SS16 exit at Fasano.   Follow signs for Pezze di Greco, and take the second right in town.

MASSERIA SALAMINA
Host: Gianvincenzo DeMiccolis Angelini
Localita: Pezze di Greco
Fasano (BA) 70121, Italy
tel: (080) 727307
8 suites with private bathrooms, 7 apartments
Lire 110,000-130,000 double B&B
All meals served
Open all year
Some English spoken
Region: Puglia

Simona and Luciano Nenna chose an idyllic location to which to relocate, surrounding themselves with hundreds of acres of woods, rivers, valleys and, best of all, utter tranquility. Eight years ago, this ambitious and hospitable couple began restoring an isolated village made up of 12 stone houses, transforming it into a rustic retreat for their exhausted friends from Rome. Besides producing all their own fruits and vegetables, their main activity is equestrian: they have 20 horses, well-equipped stables, indoor and outdoor rings, riding school and organized excursions into the scenic countryside. The "Noci" house contains seven simple rooms with bath, which retain their original terracotta floors and wood-beamed ceilings, and are decorated with country furniture. "La Terrazza," originally a hunting lodge, houses nine guestrooms with bath, including its namesake terrace room. Other buildings are "La Quercia" dining hall where guests share hearty Umbrian specialties at long tables, and the bar with huge fireplace and occasional live entertainment. Alternative activities include on-site tennis and swimming. *Directions:* Exit at Fabro from Rome-Firenze A1 autostrada. Follow signs for Parrano, turning right for La Casella before town.

LA CASELLA
Hosts: Simona & Luciano Nenna
Tenuta Valle Chiani
Ficulle (TR) 05016, Italy
tel: (0763) 86684
20 rooms, 16 with private bathrooms
Lire 75,000 per person half board
*   85,000 per person full board*
All meals served
Closed January
Fluent English spoken
Region: Umbria

Given the unbearable August heat in most parts of the country, and the inevitably overcrowded conditions at the seaside resorts during that month, it is small wonder that the cooler elevations of the Alps and Dolomites have become a favorite vacation destination for Italian families. In addition to offering the ideal atmosphere for relaxation and recharging, it offers invigorating fresh mountain air, numerous outdoor activities, spectacular scenery and, best of all, the least expensive "getaway" available in the country. The darling Merlhof bed and breakfast is owned and operated by the Kompatschers, who have created seven guestrooms within their family home in the town of Fie. The traditional, Tyrolian-style white- and dark-wood dwelling has geraniums cascading brightly from each windowsill, and looks directly onto Sciliar mountain out the back. The guestrooms are simply furnished with light pinewood beds and side tables, and only one has its own bathroom. The breakfast room overlooks the town and a small swimming pool, which is a welcome feature indeed on hot summer afternoons or after a day of hiking. *Directions:* Exit at Bolzano Nord from Verona-Brennero autostrada. Follow signs for Siusi and Fie (also called Vols) and, at main intersection, turn right to Merlhof.

MERLHOF
Hosts: Maria Kompatscher family
Via Sciliar 14
Fie allo Sciliar (Vols) (BZ) 39050, Italy
tel: (0471) 72092
7 rooms, 1 with private bathroom
Lire 25,000 per person B&B
Breakfast only
Open all year
Some English spoken (German)
Region: Alto Adige

The Hotel Aprile, owned by the Cantini Zucconi family for the past 35 years, is located in a 15th-century Medici palace behind the Piazza Santa Maria Novella, near the train station and many fine restaurants and shops. The historical building was restored under the strict ordinance of Florence's Commission of Fine Arts. The small and charming hotel is full of delightful surprises: from 16th-century paintings and a bust of the Duke of Tuscany to the frescoed breakfast room and quiet courtyard garden. The old-fashioned reception and sitting areas are invitingly furnished with Florentine renaissance antiques, comfy overstuffed red armchairs and oriental carpets. The wallpapered bedrooms include telephone and minibar, and feature parquet floors and high vaulted ceilings, but vary widely in their decor; some are too basic and modern. There are fifteen doubles with private bathrooms, and another four which share two bathrooms just outside the rooms. Request one of the quieter rooms at the back of the hotel, overlooking the garden. *Directions:* Use a detailed city map to locate the hotel, three blocks north of the Duomo. There is a parking garage.

HOTEL APRILE
Host: Valeria Cantini Zucconi
Via della Scala 6
Florence 50123, Italy
tel: (055) 216237 fax: (055) 280947
19 rooms, 15 with private bathrooms
Lire 160,000 double B&B
Breakfast only
Credit cards: all major
Open all year
Some English spoken
Region: Tuscany

If you are facing the Florence train station, a block to the right is the Via Fiume. At the end of this tranquil street is the Hotel Desiree, located on the upper floors of a building (as is typical of city pensione) and owned and operated by gracious Graziella Pili. Twenty double rooms are contained within, off a long, gleaming marble hallway wide enough to include a desk and two overstuffed armchairs. Each room has a new bathroom, high ceiling, patterned, polished tile floor, TV and telephone. The guestrooms are simply decorated with painted furniture and the occasional antique. From the small entrance area, stained glass doors lead to the sweet breakfast room with its pink linen tablecloths topped with fresh bouquets, and on out to its flower-laden balcony overlooking the famous terracotta rooftops of Florence, among them that belonging to the glorious Duomo. Signora Pili takes visible pride in her newly renovated hotel and keeps it in immaculate condition. The two-star Hotel Desiree maintains high standards and an economical rate, a combination that is not easy to find. *Directions:* Use a detailed city map to locate. Parking facilities are available.

HOTEL DESIREE
Host: Signora Graziella Pili
Via Fiume 20
Florence 50123, Italy
tel: (055) 2382382
20 rooms with private bathrooms
Lire 115,000 double B&B
Breakfast only
Open all year
Some English spoken
Region: Tuscany

It is not hard to find accommodations in a 15th-century palace in downtown Florence; the historical center of the city has little else. The Residenza is no exception, but it features the added attraction of being situated on Florence's most elegant street, the Tornabuoni. For the last three generations the cordial Giancalone family has owned the palazzo's top three floors and operated them as a pensione (now a hotel). An antique elevator takes you up to the reception area which gives onto a pretty dining room with pink tablecloths and shelves lined with a collection of bottles, vases and ceramics. Thirteen comfortably worn, simple and tastefully furnished rooms are divided between the next two floors (the upper floor being the most desirable), capped with a rooftop terrace burgeoning with flowerpots and surrounded by city views. A comfortable sitting room with high, beamed ceilings and a television for guests is located on the upper floor. La Residenza is one of the few small hotels offering dinner on the premises, and the proprietors are justifiably proud of their reputation for serving authentic Florentine cuisine. *Directions:* Use a detailed city map to locate the hotel in the heart of Florence.

LA RESIDENZA
Hosts: Gianna & Paolo (son) Giacalone
Via Tornabuoni 8
Florence 50123, Italy
tel: (055) 284197
13 rooms with private bathrooms
Lire 150,000 double B&B
Breakfast and dinner served
Credit cards: all major
Open all year
English spoken well
Region: Tuscany

The newly refurbished Hotel Silla is located on the left bank of the Arno River opposite Santa Croce, the famous 13th-century square and church where Michelangelo and Galileo are buried. This position offers views from some of the rooms, including several of Florence's most notable architectural attractions: the Duomo, the Ponte Vecchio and the tower of Palazzo Vecchio. Housed on the second and third floors of a lovely 15th-century palazzo with courtyard entrance, twenty nine spotless double rooms with private baths are pleasantly decorated with simple dark wood furniture and matching bedspreads and curtains. The fancy cream-color reception area is appointed in 17th-century Venetian style, with period furniture, chandelier and large paintings. Breakfast is served on the splendid and spacious outdoor terrace on the second floor or in the dining room overlooking the Arno. The Silla is a friendly, convenient and quiet hotel, near the Pitti Palace, leather artisan shops and many restaurants. It offers tourists a good value in pricey Florence. *Directions:* Refer to a detailed city map to locate the hotel.

HOTEL SILLA
Hosts: Avelino family
Via dei Renai 5
Florence 50125, Italy
tel: (055) 2342888 fax: (055) 2341437
29 rooms with private bathrooms
Lire 142,000 double B&B
Breakfast only
Credit cards: all major
Open all year
English spoken well
Region: Tuscany

The Hotel Splendor is exactly as its name implies: splendid. Traffic- and street noise is a common problem in the bustling urban center of Florence, but the Splendor, off on a quiet side street, manages to miss most of it. Yet guests won't miss being able to walk almost everywhere, since the hotel is only three blocks from the Duomo and near the Accademia museum where the David is found. The prim, centuries-old palazzo, of the pale-yellow hue characteristic of Florence, has geranium-filled boxes at every window. The ambience is reminiscent of a time-worn elegant private home (which the palazzo was until 1957), with its frescoed foyer and sitting rooms graced with portraits, chandeliers, overstuffed armchairs and oriental carpets. The twenty three spacious guestrooms with baths have the same flavor, although they vary greatly in decor, and some are too obviously modern. Perhaps the architectural highlight is the breakfast room, with high ceilings, parquet floors and frescoed panels all around. French doors lead from this area to an outdoor terrace with white iron chairs and tables from which guests may enjoy a lovely view of San Marco church. According to the friendly staff, this exceptionally priced hotel expects to receive another star by April, when it will adjust its rates accordingly. *Directions:* Rely on a detailed city map to locate the hotel.

HOTEL SPLENDOR
Hosts: Masoero family
Via San Gallo 30
Florence 50129, Italy
tel: (055) 483427 fax: (055) 481276
23 rooms with private bathrooms
Lire 110,000 double B&B
Breakfast only
Open all year
English spoken well
Region: Tuscany

On the hillside above Florence famous for its fantastic city views is one of the many beautiful properties pertaining to the noble Corsini family.   This particular estate is made up of an enormous castle, smaller villas, a convent, individual houses for the servants, and hundreds of acres of olive groves and hilly countryside (including Monte Cerceri where Da Vinci conducted his experiments with flight).   The 15th-century castle, where scenes from *Room with a View* were filmed, is rented out for weddings and special occasions.   Its enclosed front lawn provides a superb view over the unique rooftops of Florence.   The family is in the process of restoring the convent and smaller houses to accommodate guests, and currently offers three suite-apartments for weekly stays.   Simple, more basic rooms are available, but the superior one has a large living/dining area with upstairs loft/bedroom and a kitchenette tastefully decorated with antiques and personal belongings of the family.   An excellent restaurant on the property serves typical Florentine dishes, while a small grocery store on site sells enough of the farm's own fresh produce (cheese, wine, olive oil) to prepare a simple self-catered meal.   *Directions:* From Florence follow signs for Fiesole.   Cross through downtown and start descent back to Florence on villa-lined road.   The Maiano is on the first curve on left.

FATTORIA DI MAIANO
Hosts: Francesco Fulcis and Lucrezia Corsini
Via Benedetto da Maiano 11
Fiesole (FI) 50014, Italy
tel: (055) 599600
3 suite-apartments
Lire 75,000 per person
Trattoria on premises
Open all year
Fluent English spoken
Region: Tuscany

The Castello di Tornano is a very special place to stay for those wishing to explore in depth the rich culture of this extraordinary region. The strategically situated hilltop tower, dating back almost 1,000 years, has a 360-degree vista of the surrounding valley and has been of great historical significance during the seemingly endless territorial battles between the Siena and Florence. Given how ancient the property is, it is incredible to discover that the current owners, the Selvolini family from Florence, are only the third proprietors. Patrizia and Barbara, the family's lovely daughters, opened the wine estate to guests just three years ago. Weekly stays begin with a cocktail party around the exquisite pool cut into the rock and spanned by a bridge. Seven simply appointed suites, each with living area, kitchen, one or two bedrooms and garden, are situated in a stone farmhouse in front of the tower. The pièce de résistance, however, is the three-floor apartment within the monumental tower, impeccably furnished in grand style and featuring three bedrooms, two living rooms with fireplace, dining room, kitchen and tower-top terrace with a view not easily forgotten. Meals can be taken at the restaurant on the property. *Directions:* From Siena follow signs for Gaiole. Just past Lecchi turnoff (on left), turn right for Tornano-Guarnelotto Ristorante.

CASTELLO DI TORNANO
Hosts: Patrizia & Barbara Selvolini
Localita: Lecchi
Gaiole in Chianti (SI) 53013, Italy
tel: (0577) 746067 fax: (055) 688918
8 apartments
Lire 550,000 to 2,450,000 (tower) weekly
Trattoria on premises
Open Easter-October and Christmas
English spoken very well
Region: Tuscany

Traveling south along the heel of Italy, you will encounter a wealth of natural beauty, although, because we are far off the beaten trail, few really charming places to stay. The Masseria lo Prieno is run by the delightful Castriota family, who has owned the farm for three generations. The Castriota's crops are representative of the staples of the Apulia region, and include olives, almonds, fruits and grains. Spartan accommodations are offered in bungalows scattered among the pine woods and palms on the family property. Each guest house includes two bedrooms, kitchen, bathroom and an eating area containing basic necessities. What were formerly animal stalls have been converted into a large dining space rustically decorated with antique farm tools and brass pots. Along with warm hospitality, the family makes the offerings of the kitchen a top priority. For an exquisite and authentic traditional meal, the restaurant here is incomparable. Both Maria Grazia, the energetic daughter who runs the show, and her charming mother take pride in demonstrating how local specialties are prepared: from fresh pastas to breads and desserts. Dinner here is truly something special. *Directions:* From Taranto take N174 to Galatone, then follow signs for Secli. Turn right on Via Gramsci, then left on Via San Luca. Follow signs for lo Prieno.

MASSERIA LO PRIENO
Hosts: Castriota family
Localita: Contrada Orelle
Galatone (LE) 73044, Italy
tel: (0833) 861391/865443
9 bungalows
Lire 50,000 per person half board
All meals served
Open all year
Some English spoken
Region: Apulia

For the fortunate travelers with time to explore the rich treasures of Florence and the spectacular surrounding countryside as well, innumerable surprises await them. On the extreme outskirts of the city, the Fattoressa offers the ideal location for this type of "dual" exploration.   One of the many marvelous attractions of Florence is how the countryside comes right up to the doors of the city. Just behind the magnificent Certosa monastery is situated the 15th-century stone farmhouse of the delightfully congenial Fusi-Borgioli family. With loving care, they have transformed the farmer's quarters into guest accommodations: four sweetly simple bedrooms, each with its own spotless bathroom. Running a bed and breakfast seems to come naturally to Angelina and Amelio, who treat their guests like family and, as a result, enjoy receiving some of them year after year.   Visitors take meals *en famille* at long tables in the cozy, rustic dining room with large stone fireplace. Here Angelina proudly serves authentic Florentine specialties using ingredients from her own garden. *Directions:* Entering Florence from Certosa exit off Siena superstrada, turn left after one street.   Watch for Essegi sign just beyond bridge and turn right.

PODERE LA FATTORESSA
Hosts: Angelina Fusi & Amelio Borgioli
Via Volterrana 58
Galluzzo (FI) 50124, Italy
tel: (055) 2048418
4 rooms with private bathrooms
Lire 100,000 double B&B
Breakfast and dinner served
Open all year
No English spoken
Region: Tuscany

Cozy accommodations are hard to come by in the beautiful lake area of Garda, so it was a particular pleasure to discover the utterly delightful Ca'Vescova bed and breakfast, lovingly owned and operated by young ex-urbanites Fabio, Monica and darling son Davide. The salmon-colored farmhouse sits peacefully on a hillside surrounded by vineyards and a panorama of the lake and the quaint town of Garda below. Guests have a separate entrance to the seven small rooms on the second and third floors. All bedrooms have modern bathrooms, and are simply decorated with country antiques and old-world prints. Breakfast is served either on the flowered terrace or in the polished country-style dining room, accented by colorful ceramic cups and pitchers lining the shelves and fireplace mantle. Besides being an excellent horsewoman and gardener, Monica is a outstanding cook and demonstrates her abilities to half- and full-board guests. Just 45 km north of Verona, this is an excellent base for touring the Veneto region. *Directions:* From Verona take either the scenic lakeside route to Garda or the direct A22 autostrada toward Brennero and exit at Affi-Garda. Follow signs for Costermano, pass through town to stop light, then turn right on Via Per Marciaga.

CA'VESCOVA
Hosts: Fabio & Monica Russo
Via Per Marciago 14
Garda (VR) 37016, Italy
tel: (045) 7255057
7 rooms with private bathrooms
Lire 75,000 double B&B
*   60,000 per person half board*
Breakfast and dinner served
Open Easter-October
English spoken well
Region: Veneto

Set deep in the heart of the Chianti region, this rambling white villa with terracotta roof dominates the surrounding valley of olive trees and grape vines. Arminio Gericke, a Tuscan of German origin, made his home here over 25 years ago, and is as dedicated to the art of producing fine wines and olive oil as he is to providing impeccable hospitality to his guests. Arminio has managed to retain the villa's 18th-century character, splendidly visible in the high-ceiling, frescoed salon with piano and fireplace. In one wing are found the eight bedrooms, four with private bath, and each decorated differently with wrought-iron beds and original antiques. Also within the villa are five spacious apartments accommodating two to eight people and available by the week. Breakfast is taken downstairs in the rustic dining room off the large kitchen with cook-in fireplace. Just before the villa is a group of stone houses containing *La Cantinetta* restaurant offering excellent farm-fresh specialties. An extra plus is the picturesque swimming pool surrounded by olive trees. Tennis, horseback riding and golf are available nearby. *Directions:* Take Tavernelle exit off the Siena-Firenze superstrada. Follow signs for Passignano and, just after the abbey, turn right on a gravel road and follow signs to Rignana (12 km).

FATTORIA DI RIGNANA
Hosts: Dottor Arminio Gericke
Localita: Rignana
Greve in Chianti (FI) 50022, Italy
tel: (055) 852065　fax: (O55) 598729
8 rooms, 4 with private bathrooms, 5 apartments
Lire 70,000 double B&B
Trattoria on premises
Open Easter-October
English spoken very well
Region: Tuscany

What happens when four young and ambitious Italian men from various regions of the country pool their earnings and restaurant experience to open a country inn? You can see for yourself by visiting the recently opened Borgo Antico. In the rugged back hills of Chianti, at the highest peak of Monte San Michele, is a cluster of stone houses dating from 1300 that the energetic foursome is gradually and meticulously restoring according to antique drawings. Naturally they began with the restaurant, which emphasizes fine cuisine prepared from the freshest ingredients. Claudio and Eralio busily create in the kitchen, while Massimo and Walter host the three intimate dining rooms accented with crisp pink tablecloths. During the warmer months, regulars know to request the outdoor terrace with grape arbor overlooking the brilliant green landscape. Four guest rooms have been fashioned in the tower (one per floor, with bathrooms just outside each), and four more are to be added by the end of the year. The rooms are simply but tastefully appointed with antique armoires and colorful floral bedspreads. *Directions:* Take Incisa exit off the Florence-Siena highway. Follow signs for Greve and, after 14 km, turn left for Lucolena/Monte San Michele.

LOCANDA BORGO ANTICO
Hosts: Claudio, Walter, Massimo, Eralio
Localita: Locolena
Greve in Chianti (FI) 50022, Italy
tel: (055) 851024
4 rooms with private bathrooms
Lire 55,000 double B&B
All meals served (closed Tuesdays)
Credit cards: all major
Open Easter-November
English spoken well
Region: Tuscany

The Azienda Zanella gets the prize for most original location, and what it lacks in charm, its proprietors make up for in hospitality. Belonging to the Zanella family, the farm is situated on a remote island in the Venice lagoon, containing a minuscule town with a restaurant, church and two stores, surrounded by cultivated fields. Accessible solely by boat, a stay here reveals a more authentic lifestyle than that on display in Venice, jaded from centuries of tourism. Beyond a wall of cypress and up a stone path is an ivy-covered, white farmhouse with a terracotta roof. The entry leads directly into the restaurant, featuring a veranda and long, rustic wooden tables. This is a favorite spot with local families, who gather here on Sundays for a traditional multi-course meal of farm-fresh dishes including duck, rabbit and garden vegetables. Upstairs, overlooking the garden, are the two guestrooms, immaculate but uninspired, with modern, dark wood furniture. For travelers touring Veneto, the farm offers a unique and economical alternative to the high price of accommodation in Venice. *Directions:* Take the #13 ferry from Venice to Murano. San Erasmo-Chiesa is the fourth stop. Call ahead to be met or plan on a 1 km walk past the cemetery to the Zanella farm.

AZIENDA ZANELLA
Hosts: Zanella family
Via Forti 16
Isola di San Erasmo
Venice 30101, Italy
tel: (041) 5285329
2 rooms, 1 with private bathroom
Lire 40,000 per person full board
All meals served
Open all year
No English spoken
Region: Veneto

Just south of the fascinating etruscan/medieval villages of Montemerano, Sovana and Saturnia (well-known for the 2,000-year-old hot springs), is this isolated B&B situated within a national park.   A cluster of stone buildings there, neglected for decades, was once a community serving the castle down the road.   This is where two extraordinarily determined Dutch women decided to settle, and the results of their renovating efforts are truly miraculous.   Five guestrooms have been tastefully fashioned in one part of the sectioned farmhouse, each with its own distinct personality and color scheme.   Special marbling techniques have been applied to the walls in warm earth tones, lending an intimate feeling to the rooms. Antique furniture mixes well with wicker pieces, enhanced by the rich terracotta floors and beamed ceilings.   A minor dilemma of how to make a windowless passageway appealing was resolved by importing an Austrian surrealistic painter to fresco the walls, floor, and ceiling.   The trompe d'oeil effect is like walking onto a terrace on a romantic starry night.   Other amenities include a cozy kitchen and a library for guests.   *Directions:* From Rome (1-1/2 hours away), take the Aurelia road to Vulci, follow signs for Manciano.   Campigliola is on the left, 12 km before town.

CAMPIGLIOLA COUNTRY CLUB
Hosts: Frida Van Der Horst & P.J. VanDen Bergh
Localita: Campigliola
Manciano (GR) 58014, Italy
tel: (0564) 629194
5 rooms with private bathrooms
Lire 102,000 double B&B; 120,000 triple B&B
Breakfast only
Open all year
English spoken well
Region: Tuscany

When the parents of Florentine sisters Francesca and Beatrice Baccetti proposed to let them take over the family's country home and vineyards and convert the property into a B&B, they eagerly accepted the challenge. Restoration work began immediately on the two adjacent stone buildings dating back to 1400. All original architectural features were preserved, leaving the five guestrooms and five apartments (for 2 to 4 people) with clay-tiled floors, wood-beamed ceilings, mansard roofs, and generous views over the tranquil Tuscan countryside. The comfortable and tidy rooms are furnished with good reproductions and feel almost hotel-like, with telephone, television and modern bathrooms in each. A swimming pool, tennis courts and nearby horse stables are activities at the guests' disposal, although finding enough to do is hardly a problem with Florence only 24 km away. Lingering over breakfast, served at wood tables in the stone-walled dining room (or out on the terrace), allows the opportunity to chat with either Francesca or Beatrice, both very outgoing and knowledgeable on their native area. *Directions:* From Florence take the superstrada toward Siena, exiting at San Casciano Nord. Follow signs for town, taking a left at the sign for Mercatale. Salvadonica is on this road and well-marked.

SALVADONICA
Hosts: Francesca & Beatrice Baccetti
Via Grevigiana 82
Mercatale Val di Pesa (FI) 50024, Italy
tel: (055) 8218039 fax: (055) 8218043
5 rooms with private bathrooms, 5 apartments
Lire 100,000 double B&B
Breakfast only
Open March-October
English spoken very well
Region: Tuscany

While many agriturismo farms are run by transplanted urbanites, many are still owned and operated by farmers whose families have worked the land for generations. Such is the case with Onofrio Contento and his family, proprietors of Masseria Conchia, not far from the city of Monopoli and the sea. The three studious, red-headed sons (evidence of Apuglia's Norman invasion) assist their father with chores on the farm, where for five generations, the family has produced olives, almonds and cattle. Inside the main coral-color house are modest and immaculate quarters for guests, consisting presently of two two-bedroom apartments with kitchens, one double with bath, and two doubles sharing a bath. Old and new family furniture has been combined to decorate the rooms. The view is pleasingly pastoral, overlooking olive-studded hills. Several new rooms are currently under construction in a nearby building overlooking a lovely stone-walled garden and fruit orchard. Breakfast and extra meals are taken together with the family in their dining room. Recommended for visitors with some command of the Italian language. *Directions:* Seventy km from Brindisi. Take coastal route N16, exiting at Monopoli-San Francesco. Take road back across highway and make first left. Follow the road for 2 km to the pink house.

MASSERIA CONCHIA
Hosts: Onofrio Contento family
Contrada Cristo delle Zolle 227
Monopoli (BA) 70043, Italy
tel: (080) 777472/748560
5 rooms with private bathrooms, 2 apartments
Lire 50,000 double B&B
Breakfast only
Open all year
Very little English spoken
Region: Apuglia

More than a cursory visit to the culturally rich region of Veneto, with its Palladio villas and enchanting towns such as Verona, Vicenza and Padua, will handsomely reward the effort. Just south of Padua, outside the medieval town of Monselice with its imposing castle, is the family-run B&B of Silvia Sagradin and family. Ten years ago they restored the late-19th-century farmhouse, converting the stables into a large airy restaurant equipped with long family-style wooden tables and copper pots hanging from the ceiling. Judging from the number of patrons, it is apparent that the eatery has become a favorite Sunday outing for both rural and urban folk, largely due to the superior country cuisine served there. The entire family is involved in the effort, either as hosts, working in the fruit orchards, or on site in the busy kitchen, where it seems fresh pasta is being prepared at all hours. For guests wishing to stay overnight, two rooms have recently been incorporated into the house. Ideal for a family of four, this separate section of the house includes the two bedrooms (decorated with inherited country furniture, lace curtains and beamed ceilings) newly built bathroom and a small private dining area. *Directions:* Take the A13 autostrada south toward Ferrara, exiting at Monselice, then follow the yellow signs to Molini.

FATTORIA SAVELLON MOLINI
Hosts: Silvia Sagradin & family
Via Savellon Molini
Monselice (PD) 35042, Italy
tel: (0429) 73135
2 rooms sharing a bathroom
Lire 25,000 per person B&B
All meals served
Open Easter-October
No English spoken
Region: Veneto

Traveling southwest toward Florence through the foothills of the Appenines, the scenery transforms itself dramatically from the flatlands of the *padana* into soft green hills textured with alternating fields of wheat and grape vines. From Bologna, the Tenuta Bonzara farm and vineyard is a half hour drive up a road that winds through scented pine forest, arriving at a group of houses owned by several farming families. The wine estate is owned by Dottore Lambertini of Bologna, and is run by warm-hearted Mario and his family, whose main responsibility is overseeing the wine production. Guest accommodation on the estate consists of two small houses containing two apartments each with one or two bedrooms, bathroom, kitchenette and sitting room. Preferred are the one-bedroom apartments in the older house with small corner fireplaces, red-brick floors and beamed ceilings, rustically furnished with simple pinewood pieces. A trattoria on the premises serves meals, and an interesting museum has been set up in the old barn displaying antique farm tools, carts, and agricultural machines. Horseback riding is available, and participation in the grape harvesting is encouraged. *Directions:* Take Bologna/Casalecchio exit from the A1 autostrada, and continue to Gesso, Rivabella and Monte San Pietro, where you go left up the hill.

TENUTA BONZARA
Host: Dottor Angelo Lambertini
Via San Chierlo 37
Monte San Pietro (BO) 40050, Italy
tel: (051) 933.547/225.772
4 apartments
Lire 450,000 weekly
Trattoria on premises (dinner only)
Open Easter-October
Some English spoken
Region: Emilia-Romagna

The scenic approach to the Fattoria di Vibio passes through lush green hills, by picturesque farms, and is highlighted by a romantic view of the quaint town of Todi 20 km away, setting the mood for an enjoyable stay. This is a top-drawer bed and breakfast consisting of several recently restored stone houses, and manning the operation are two young, handsome brothers from Rome. The houses sit side by side and share between them ten double rooms with private bath. Common areas for guests include a cozy, country-style living room with fireplace, game room and country kitchen. The accommodations are enhanced by preserved architectural features such as terracotta floors and exposed-beam ceilings. Typical Umbrian handicrafts like wrought-iron beds, renovated antiques, and Deruta ceramics are in evidence. On the assumption that guests may find it difficult to leave this haven, the hosts offer full-board, along with swimming, tennis, hiking and horseback riding. Signora Saladini, with a passion for cooking, gets all the richly deserved credit for the marvelous meals served either poolside or on the panoramic terrace. *Directions:* From either Todi or Orvieto follow route SS448 until turnoff for Vibio just outside Todi. Follow well-marked dirt road for 10 km.

FATTORIA DI VIBIO
Hosts: Giuseppe & Filippo Saladini
Localita: Buchella-Doglio
Montecastello di Vibio (PG) 06057, Italy
tel: (075) 8780370/8749607
10 rooms with private bathrooms
Lire 86,000--100,000 per person full board
two-day minimum (weekly only mid-June/mid-September)
All meals served
Open Easter-November
Very little English spoken
Region: Umbria

Surprisingly, one of the least visited regions in Italy is the Marches, an area rich in culture, nature and history, bordering the Adriatic on one side and Emilia-Romangna, Umbria and Abruzzo on the other. Just 15 km from the coast in the heart of this soft, hilly countryside, is the Campana farm, run by 10 families of professionals and artists (architect, painter, designer, poet, doctor) who came here from Milan 10 years ago in search of an alternative lifestyle. The farm, made up of four pale-peach stone houses dating from 1700, has been restored with great care and taste, making space for private quarters, a refined restaurant, wine cellar, studio, music room and, for guests, one double room and two suites. The suites have lovely terraces looking across vineyard-covered hills to the distant sea, and are decorated with a combination of old and new furnishings. Drawing on the considerable pool of available talent, an unusual variety of activities is offered: from courses in painting, theater, sculpture and photography to workshops in crafting leather, silk and wool. *Directions:* From Ancona go south on the A14 autostrada, exit at Pedaso and continue south to Carassai, then turn right. After 5 km, turn right for Montefiore, then left at the small sign for La Campana.

LA CAMPANA
Hosts: Coop Agricola
Via Menocchia 39
Montefiore d'Aso (AP) 63010, Italy
tel: (0734) 938.229
1 room and 2 suites with private bathrooms
Lire 60,000 double B&B
Breakfast and dinner served
Open all year
English spoken well
Region: Marches

La Loggia, built in 1427 at the height of the Renaissance, is the oldest wine estate in Chianti. It was purchased 12 years ago and meticulously restored by Guilio Baruffaldi (formerly an art dealer) and his wife Cuca Roaldi, who moved here from Milan. They have succeeded in reviving the estate's splendor while respecting its past, enhancing its architectural beauty while giving utmost attention to comforts and warmth. Their commitment to perfect hospitality is evident in the care given to the decor of the apartment-suites, each containing one to three bedrooms, living room, kitchen, fireplace and many lovely antiques and objects from the Baruffaldi's own art collection. Apart from basking in the pure romance and tranquility of this unpretentious place, there is a swimming pool, horseback riding, nearby tennis and golf. Other activities include the occasional cooking or wine lesson, and impromptu dinners in the cellar. The host and their absolutely charming administrative assistant, Ivana, seem to exist merely to pamper their guests' every whim. This is the stuff dreams are made of. *Directions:* From the Florence-Siena autostrada exit after Casciano at Bargino. Turn right at end of ramp, then left for Montefiridolfi (5 km). La Loggia is just outside town.

FATTORIA LA LOGGIA
Hosts: Giulio Baruffaldi & Cuca Roaldi
Via Collina, Montefiridolfi
San Casciano Val di Pesa (FI) 50020, Italy
tel: (055) 8244288 fax: (055) 8244283
10 suite-apartments
Lire 160,000-500,000 daily per apartment
   minimum stay 3 days (1 week high season)
No breakfast, occasional dinner served
Open all year
Fluent English spoken
Region: Tuscany

A destination as special as the *maremma*, or southern Tuscany, can be kept secret for just so long. One response to increasing interest in its singular attractions is the opening or expansion of several noteworthy places to stay. The Villa Acquaviva, once owned by nobility, has been a small family hotel for the past seven years. The young and ambitious proprietors, Serafino and Valentina, completed extensive remodeling, to include seven guestrooms named for and painted in the colors of local wildflowers. The bedrooms all have private baths, and are decorated with country antiques and wrought-iron beds. The charming breakfast room has sky-blue tablecloths and looks out through arched glass to a lush flower garden with alternating palms and umbrella pines, and on to a view over the gently rolling landscape up to the village of Montemerano, a quaint, medieval town with excellent restaurants and artisan shops. Breakfast of homemade cakes, breads and jams can be taken in or out on the patio. The hosts also produce both red and white wine and olive oil, and by this summer will produce another 10 rooms within a stone farmhouse just in front of the peach-colored villa. *Directions:* From Rome, take the Aurelia road, exiting at Vulci. Follow signs for Manciano, then for Montemerano. Approximately 1-1/2 hours from Rome.

VILLA ACQUAVIVA
Hosts: Valentina & Serafino D'Ascenzi
Strada Scansanese
Montemerano (GR) 58050, Italy
tel: (0564) 602890
7 rooms with private bathrooms
Lire 100,000 double B&B
Breakfast only
Open March-December
Some English spoken
Region: Tuscany

For four generations the Laudomia has been an immensely popular mealtime stop for daytrippers in picturesque southern Tuscany, serving exquisite fresh-pasta dishes among other delicacies. So it made sense for Clara Casolaro and her daughter Roberta to add guestrooms so that visitors could linger and take full advantage of their warm hospitality. In fact, once travelers discover this delightful combination of authentic regional cuisine, comfortable accommodations and unspoiled scenery, they become regulars. Rooms across the street from the restaurant all have private baths and are simply but tastefully decorated with scattered antiques and bright floral bedspreads. The rooms off the roadside are quieter and offer lovely views across the rolling olive-tree-dotted hills. It is a memorable treat to dine in an intimate corner of the restaurant (filled with family antiques and artwork), especially if you put yourself completely in the Clara's competent hands. A grape-arbor garden in back is a delightful spot to relax on a summer evening. In the vicinity are the thermal hot springs of Saturnia and many intriguing medieval towns, including Pitigliano, seemingly carved out of the limestone cliff. *Directions:* From Rome, take the Aurelia road north, turning off at Vulci. Follow signs for Manciano, then Montemerano. From Siena, take the superstrada to Grosseto. Follow signs for Scansano, then Montemerano.

LOCANDA LAUDOMIA
Hosts: Clara Casolaro & Roberta Detti
Poderi di Montemerano (GR) 58050, Italy
tel: (0564) 620062/620013
12 rooms with private bathrooms
Lire 55,000 double B&B
All meals served
Open all year
Very little English spoken
Region: Tuscany

Lucia Ana Luhan, whose parents came from Italy, grew up in a family rich in Italian tradition.   She now lives in southern California, is married to a busy surgeon, has a family of three and operates several successful fresh pasta restaurants plus a catering service.   Such activity would keep most women more than occupied, but not Lucia.   While on holiday in Italy a few year ago, she fell in love with a 500-year-old stone farmhouse, bought it on a whim, and converted it into the Bed & Breakfast of Tuscany.   Now Lucia commutes back and forth between California and Italy.   When Lucia is not at her Italian farmhouse, it is well-managed by Renata Cerchiari who lives there all year.   This seven bedroom inn is not luxurious, nor is it meant to be.   All of the rooms are decorated in a homey, comfortable way; nothing contrived, just naturally pleasing and in keeping with the rustic nature of the old stone farmhouse.   When the weather is mild, a bountiful breakfast is served outside on the terrace where guests congregate again in the late afternoon to sip cool drinks while sharing their day's adventures.   In the evening, if requested, a simple supper of homemade soup, cheeses and cold cuts is available. Or, for guests who want a fancier dinner, the famous spa town of Montecatini is just a six-minute drive down the hill.   *Directions:* From Monsummano Terme (52 km east of Florence) drive 3 km northwest, following signs to Montevettolini.

BED & BREAKFAST OF TUSCANY
Host: Lucia Ana Luhan
Via dei Bronzodi 144
Montevettolini (PT) 51010, Italy
7 rooms with private bathrooms
tel & fax: (0572) 628817
$150 double B&B (USA)
Breakfast and dinner served
Open all year
English spoken very well
Region: Tuscany

Novella and Laerte Piangatelli, delightful and gregarious hosts, have been welcoming guests into their home for over 10 years, ever since they moved to Emilia-Romangna from the south. Having agricultural experience, they were able to set up a farm, tended to by Laerte, while Novella, the town schoolteacher, oversees the kitchen. She is an excellent cook and guests return time and time again for her pasta, joining the family at the long wood table in their rustic dining room with its hanging brass pots and ox harnesses. Guest accommodations have been transferred recently from upstairs in the white 18th-century farmhouse to the horse stalls, which have been converted into eight double rooms with private baths. The rooms are immaculate, if rather plain with basic modern furnishings. Guests tend to their own rooms and are even apt to help clear the table in the very informal and *en famille* atmosphere promoted at Le Radici. The sea, just 15 km away, can be seen in the distance, and several medieval towns and castles dot the hills in the surrounding countryside. A unique experience, best enjoyed if you speak some Italian. *Directions:* On route 9 from Rimini to Cesana, follow signs for Calisese and Montiano. Turn left at Esso gas station for Le Radici.

LE RADICI
Hosts: Novella & Laerte Piangatelli
Localita: Montenovo
Via Golano 808
Montiano (OF) 47020, Italy
tel: (0547) 51001
8 room with private bathrooms
Lire 40,000 per person half board
Breakfast and dinner served
Open all year
Very little English spoken
Region: Emilia-Romangna

In the northern section of the Piedmont region, leading into the foothills of the Alps, is the peaceful countryside where Piercarlo Novares, Il Mompolino's cordial host, decided to establish his inn and equestrian center. Run more like a small hotel, the twelve guestrooms are divided between two mustard-color buildings. Each room has a private bath and balcony, and is complemented with rustic furnishings. The larger suites feature sitting rooms and are the nicest, furnished with the occasional antique. A large, open dining room serves breakfast, lunch and dinner, and boasts delectable regional dishes skillfully prepared by local women. Il Mompolino would make an ideal stopover on the way to the Alps, the lake region or Milan. It also provides an appealing spot to relax for a few days between more demanding tourist destinations. Sports activities abound, including horseback riding, tennis, swimming, and a gym with sauna. A variety of horseback-riding lessons is offered at the equestrian center, as are mounted excursions into the adjacent national park. Perhaps a good idea between bowls of pasta! *Directions:* Take the Santhia exit from the Milan-Turin A4 autostrada. Turn right for Ivrea. Follow signs for Mottalciata and Mompolino.

IL MOMPOLINO
Host: Piercarlo Novarese
Mottalciata (VC) 13030, Italy
tel: (0161) 857667
12 rooms with private bathrooms
Lire 75,000 double B&B
All meals served
Open all year
Some English spoken
Region: Piedmont

In a beautiful, unspoiled area of northern Umbria between the enchanting towns of Gubbio, Citta del Castello and Perugia, travelers are made at home in the 100-acre hillside farmhouse of the Berna family, native Romans. It is no wonder that the area, rich in Renaissance art and architecture, has become an international artist's colony, frequently organizing music festivals and art exhibits. Three small stone houses clustered together make up the Berna's property, two for guests and one for Marisa and her family who come and go from the city. Stone walls, terracotta floors and beamed ceilings lend natural charm to the rooms, while lace curtains, handsome country antiques, floral sofas and dried flower arrangements enhance the cozy ambience. Beautifully tiled bathrooms, living area and down-sized country kitchen are found in both houses, which are available for weekly rental only. In addition to being a gracious hostess, Marisa is actively involved in the community's cultural affairs and is an invaluable resource for information about the region. She also conducts week-long combination cooking and touring classes. *Directions:* From Perugia take route N3, exiting at Umbertide. Follow signs for Niccone (12 km) and turn left in town. At the next group of houses on the road, turn right up the hill the to group of three stone houses.

LA MARIDIANA
Hosts: Berna family
Niccone 173
Umbertide (PG) 06019, Italy
tel: (075) 9303234 or (06) 856166
2 houses
Lire 500-950,000 weekly
No meals served
Open all year
English spoken very well
Region: Umbria

On the border of Umbria and the Marches regions, within reach of the unforgettably romantic towns of Spoleto, Todi, Assisi and Perugia, is the 18th-century stone farmhouse of Francesco Rambotti.   The house is beautifully situated atop a hill overlooking the peaceful countryside.   Aside from wine-producing grapes, the farm occupies itself raising deer, sheep and mountain goats, which roam freely on the property.   Open for all meals, the tavern-like dining room has a fireplace, exposed-beamed ceiling, long wood tables and walls lined with wine casks. Hearty regional fare is served up here, complemented by the farm's own wine. Guest accommodation is provided within the house in four double rooms sharing two baths, or alternately, two two-bedroom apartments with bath and kitchenette. The furnishings are spartan and utilitarian, and the baths are new and immaculate. The Rambotti family also owns another hotel (the Fontemaggio) in Assisi, whose restaurant is a popular local gathering spot.   This part of the country is loaded with must-see destinations, and La Cupa-Le Valle offers an inexpensive base from which to explore this incomparable area.   *Directions:* From the Spoleto-Foligno road, turn right at La Valle after the town of Nocera.

LA CUPA
Host: Francesco Rambotti
Localita: Colle
Nocera Umbra (PG) 06021, Italy
tel: (0742) 810130
4 rooms sharing 2 bathrooms, or 2 apartments
hl 1
Lire 40,000 per person half board
All meals served
Open all year
Very little English spoken
Region: Umbria

It was a great pleasure to find such an attractive B&B spot so close to Orvieto, a fascinating and popular tourist destination, famous for its magical cathedral. The very cordial Belcapo family actually owns two adjacent farms on the outskirts of and overlooking the majestic town on its limestone perch. La Cacciata also commands a dramatic view of the rich Umbrian valley below. The 200-acre farm/vineyard, in competent Belcapo-family hands for five generations, produces top-rated Orvieto Classico on a large scale, as well as a red and a rose wine. The primary turn-of-the-century villa and one small stone house are reserved for family residences, while four other houses scattered around the property have been remodeled to accommodate guests. In the fifteen rooms, which share eight modern bathrooms, care has been taken to preserve authentic architectural features and to select refined country antiques which blend harmoniously with them. An airy dining room overlooking the countryside and horse stables serves up sumptuous dinners. A swimming pool is planned for this summer. *Directions:* From Orvieto, follow signs for Porano, turning left before town for **La Cacciata**.

LA CACCIATA
Hosts: Belcapo family
Localita: Canale
Orvieto (TR) 05018, Italy
tel: (0763) 90192/41373
15 rooms sharing 8 bathrooms
Lire 70,000 double B&B
* 55,000 per person half board*
Breakfast and dinner served
Open all year
Very little English spoken
Region: Umbria

Lo Spagnulo gives us a good picture of how the masseria farms of Apulia functioned in the 1600s. They were self-sufficient agricultural production centers, described as "factories," which included the proprietors' villa, housing for farmers, common dining area, church, administrative offices, animal shelters and work areas. Cities were dependent on these large complexes for fresh produce, meat and cheese. The Spagnulo still cultivates animals, fresh produce, almonds and olives. Fortress-like in appearance, its white-stone exterior leads inside to a courtyard garden off of which the guest quarters are located. These vary in size and shape, many comprising two or three bedrooms, living/eating area and kitchen. Featuring the vaulted ceilings, exposed beams, terracotta floors and stone walls of the original building, the rooms display charm despite the somewhat spartan furnishings. These accommodations are recommended over the nondescript rooms which have been added in a modern building nearby. The stalls have been converted into a restaurant for guests serving typical local dishes family style. Proprietor Livino Massari, a professor, and his family are present on weekends and during the summer. *Directions:* Heading south on Route 379, exit at Marina di Ostuni. Follow signs to Rosa Marina, turning left at the sign for the farm.

MASSERIA LO SPAGNULO
Host: Livino Massari
Localita: Rosa Marina
Ostuni (BR) 72017, Italy
tel: (0831) 970209/333756
12 apartments
Lire 60,000 double B&B
*   50,000 per person half board*
All meals served
Open all year
Some English spoken
Region: Apulia

It was in 1987 when Rosemarie and her husband Filippo bought and restored the elegant 16th-century Villa Montesolare (sun-colored as its name implies), opening its doors just recently to guests. Crowning a summit in unspoiled countryside between Umbria and Tuscany, just south of lovely Lake Trasimeno, the villa overlooks its surrounding estate cultivated with olive trees and grape vines. A wide grey-stone staircase leads up to the eight guestrooms and two suites, all with private bath and furnished in appropriate period style with carefully selected antiques. Across from the cozy bar at the entrance, where guests enjoy a cocktail together before dinner, is the intimate and elegant frescoed dining room, where fine Tuscan cuisine is presented under the supervision of Rosemarie. Guests are made to feel at home, whether relaxing in the impressive powder-blue upstairs salon with glass chandelier and massive stone fireplace, or wandering through the Italian Renaissance lemon- tree garden with corner chapel dating from 1500. Less passive activities include tennis, horseback riding, or swimming in the gorgeous hillside pool while awaiting an Umbrian sunset. *Directions:* From Perugia take N220 toward Citta di Pieve. After Fontignano (3 km), turn right at San Paolo which leads up to the villa.

VILLA DI MONTESOLARE
Hosts: Rosemarie & Filippo Strunk Iannarone
Panicale (PG) 06064, Italy
tel: (075) 832376
8 rooms and 2 suites with private bathrooms
Lire 98,000 per person half board
*   (114,000 high season)*
Breakfast and dinner served
Open April-November
English spoken very well
Region: Umbria

La Scuderia is beautifully situated in the heart of Tuscany, and, aside from a wonderful restaurant, offers three apartments for rent to travelers planning to spend some time touring the region.   The suite in the back is a favorite hideaway. Here you will find a plain little old-fashioned parlor, a large bathroom (with a tiny bathtub), a cheerful, well-supplied kitchen with a table tucked in the corner for dining and a romantic bedroom which is simply but attractively furnished with family antiques.   This particular apartment also features a "Romeo and Juliet" balcony overlooking the garden and vineyards.   The apartments are best-suited for a week's stay (breakfast not included in weekly rate), but guests will be taken on a B&B basis for a three-day minimum.   In the garden restaurant, owned by young local couple Rossella and Marco, visitors can enjoy a simple, delicious, home-cooked dinner (closed Wednesdays).   La Scuderia is not a sophisticated, luxurious hotel, but for those who enjoy simple accommodation and appreciate heart-felt hospitality, this is a real winner. *Directions:* Approximately 30 km south of Florence, the Scuderia is located 5 km northeast of Sambuca.

LA SCUDERIA
Hosts: Stella & Carlo Casolaro
Badia a Passignano
Sambuca Val di Pesa (FI) 50020, Italy
tel: (055) 8071524
3 apartments
Lire 80,000 double B&B (3-day minimum)
  600,000 per week (breakfast not included)
All meals served
Open all year
Very little English spoken
Region: Tuscany

Lovers of Tuscany's romantic countryside will envy the McCobbs, who after years in Rome decided to buy and restore an old stone farmhouse south of Siena and make a new home there. On the approach, at the crest of the dramatic cypress-lined drive, the visitor is rewarded with 360-degree view of the soft, green hills dotted with villages. The panorama should be appreciated upon arrival as you'll likely have trouble tearing yourself away from the luxurious comfort of the spacious guest quarters and the refreshment of the swimming pool. The five suites consist of a cozy sitting area, fireplace, writing desk, library, and amenities such as fridge, phone and complimentary wine. The decor is a harmonious mix of antiques and family memorabilia (acquired throughout their world travels) which blend perfectly with the pretty floral-chintz upholstery and color-coordinated Ralph Lauren sheets. The palatial bathrooms are worth special mention since they provide so many decadent extras: whirlpool bath, his/her marble sinks, bathrobes and plush towels. Fresh muffins and breads are served either in the atrium breakfast room or out on the terrace. A true indulgence. *Directions:* From Rome take the A1 autostrada, exiting at Chiusi. After Montepulciano, follow signs for Pienza. After 14 km watch for a small sign on the left indicating La Saracina.

LA SARACINA
Hosts: The McCobb family
Strada Statale 146, km 29.7
Pienza (SI) 53026, Italy
tel. & fax: (0578) 748022
5 suites with private bathrooms
Lire 240,000 double B&B
Breakfast only
Closed February
Fluent English spoken
Region: Tuscany

Susan and John Abbot hail from the East Coast of the United States, but they have lived in Italy for over 20 years, and it is now *home* to them. When they saw the Castello di Polgeto, it was love at first sight and, according to John, they bought it in 20 minutes. Their impulse is understandable. The castle is idyllically perched on a hillside with blissful Umbrian vistas of vineyards, olive groves, green meadows and wooded hills. When they purchased it, the castle was practically a shell: they had to install bathrooms, build proper roofs, add walls, tile the floors, wire for adequate electricity, plant artistic landscaping and on and on. It has been years of work, but John is both an artist and architect and it has come together like a dream. Six self-catering apartments, individually decorated using rustic native materials, choice country antiques and simple fabrics, are artfully integrated with modern furniture and abstract paintings. A lovely pool is tucked into a secluded terrace below the castle. By the time you arrive, Susan and John might have completed their latest addition, a wonderful suite in the ancient tower. *Directions:* Thirty km north of Perugia, the castle is 4 km southwest of Umbertide on the road marked to Preggio.

CASTELLO DI POLGETO
Hosts: Susan & John Abbot
Umbertide-Polgeto (PG) 06019, Italy
tel: (075) 9413719 fax:(075) 9413719
6 apartments
£400-465 (UK) per week
3-night minimum, weekly stays preferred
Reservations only through Harrison-Stanton/London
Res tel: UK (071) 7365094 fax: UK (071) 3842327
No meals served
Open all year - No children under 16
Fluent English spoken
Region: Umbria

Forty five km northeast of Florence, in a beautiful, hilly area of Tuscany, is the Rufina valley, famous for the robust red wine of the same name. Crowning a wooded slope here is one of the many residences of the noble Galeotti-Ottieri family. The 15th-century main villa, where the family lives when not in Florence, was once a convent. The interior reveals spacious high-ceilinged halls with frescoes depicting family history. The family is also in the process of restoring several stone farmhouses on the vast property, one of which is the Locanda Praticino, whose upper floor contains eight lovely and simple double rooms, each with private bath and named after the color scheme they display. Downstairs is found a large dining and living room with vaulted ceiling, enormous stone fireplace and family antiques. A unique loft bedroom in the third-floor cupola offers a sweeping view of the lush countryside. Available for longer stays are five very tastefully decorated apartments (two in the main house). The Petrognano is a tranquil spot where guests may enjoy the gracious hospitality of a family whose ancestors played an important role in Florentine history. *Directions:* From Florence head toward Pontassieve. Continue to Rufina, turning right at Castiglioni-Pomino. The farm is just before Pomino.

FATTORIA PETROGNANO
Host: Cecilia Galeotti Ottieri
Localita: Pomino
Rufina (FI) 50060, Italy
tel: (055) 8318812
8 rooms with private bathrooms, 5 apartments
Lire 80,000 double B&B
All meals served
Open all year
Little English spoken
Region: Tuscany

Elena and Cesare Taticchi heartily welcome guests to their tobacco and horse-breeding farm above Perugia.   The roadside approach to this rambling renaissance villa is deceptive, as its beauty faces *in* to the interior garden.   The former stables near the main house contain a breakfast room and eight guestrooms with wood-beamed ceilings, brick floors and are sweetly furnished in simple country style. Ceramic bathroom tile (and lamps), handmade by their talented daughter, depict horses, ducks, roses, butterflies and the like, for which the rooms are named.   The main villa's dramatic entrance foyer with arched stairway leads up to a glassed-in veranda overlooking a lush flower garden and woods through which the Tiber River flows. Elena serves her specialties in the elegant old-style dining room with chandelier and frescoes. Time stands still in the wonderfully cluttered library/billiard room, as well as the two living rooms with grand piano, oriental carpets and period paintings.   Twenty horses are available for lessons in the indoor/outdoor ring or excursions in the area.   *Directions:* Take route E45 from Perugia and exit at Ponte Pattoli. Turn right at "T" intersection and continue for 1 km.   Farm is just after tennis/sport complex (open to B&B guests).

IL COVONE
Hosts: Elena & Cesare Taticchi
Strada della Fratticiola 2
Ponte Pattoli (PG) 06080, Italy
tel: (075) 694140 fax: (075) 694493
8 rooms with private bathrooms
Lire 90-110,000 per person half board
*   3-day minimum stay*
Breakfast and dinner served
Open all year
Very little English spoken
Region: Umbria

The Vecchio Convento is a real gem, offering quality accommodation for a moderate price.   Its several dining rooms are brimming with rustic country charm and serve delicious meals prepared from local produce.   There are nine guest rooms, each with a private bathroom and tastefully decorated with antiques.   The town of Portico di Romagna is, like the inn, inviting yet unpretentious: an old village surrounded by wooded hills and clear mountain streams.   A stroll through medieval pathways that twist down between the weathered stone houses leads you to an ancient stone bridge gracefully arching over a rushing stream.   The inn too is old.   It was not, as you might expect given its name, originally a convent. According to its gracious owner, Marisa Raggi, it was named for a restaurant located in a convent that she and her husband, Giovanni (the chef), used to operate. When they moved here they kept the original name.   The restaurant (closed Wednesdays) is still their primary focus, as its fine, fresh cuisine reflects.   Due to the winding, two-lane mountain highway which leads to the village, it takes about two hours to drive the 75 km from Florence, but if you enjoy the adventure of exploring Italy's back roads, this small hotel will certainly become one of your favorites.   *Directions:*   The inn is located 34 km southwest of the town of Forli.

ALBERGO AL VECCHIO CONVENTO
Hosts: Marisa Raggi & Giovanni Cameli
Via Roma 7
Portico di Romagna (OF) 47010, Italy
tel: (0543) 967752 fax: (0543) 967877
9 rooms with private bathrooms
Lire 90,000 double B&B
All meals served (closed Wednesdays)
Credit cards: AX DC VS
Open all year
Some English spoken
Region: Emilia-Romagna

On the outskirts of historical Mantua is the Villa Schiarino, one of the magnificent estates formerly belonging to the Gonzaga family, once among the most powerful nobility in Lombardy.   The cordial Eliseo family, the present owners, have taken on the enormous task of restoring the 15th-century palace room by room.   With high vaulted ceilings, completely frescoed rooms, wrought-iron chandeliers and original terracotta floors, the seemingly endless parade of rooms reveal one delight after another.   Besides being a museum, the villa is also used for large parties, weddings, and business affairs.   Surrounding the villa are small houses, once inhabited by the farm hands, which are now available to travelers on a weekly basis.   The three modest but spacious and comfortable apartments are equipped with kitchens and appointed with a mixture of antique and contemporary furniture. This location is the ideal spot to base yourself while exploring less-touristy Ferrara, Cremona, Verona and Mantua, which is filled with medieval and renaissance buildings (Palazzo del Te and Palazzo Ducale are must-sees).   *Directions:* From Mantua take route N62 past the church and turn left on Via Gramsci.   Follow for 1 km to the villa.

VILLA SCHIARINO LENA
Hosts: Lena Eliseo family
Via Santa Maddalena 7
Porto Mantovano (MN) 46047, Italy
tel: (0376) 398238
3 apartments
Lire 600,000-850,000 weekly
No meals served
Open all year
English spoken well
Region: Lombardy

High above the strip of shore holding the Fortino Napoleonico hotel sits the Hotel Emilia, owned by the Fiorini Dubbini family.   Grandmother Emilia opened a small restaurant right on the beach 40 years ago, subsequently gaining an excellent reputation for fresh seafood dishes.   That successful undertaking was succeeded by the hotel (which, not surprisingly, has a restaurant strong on seafood), surrounded by an extensive lawn sweeping to the edge of a cliff that drops 150 meters straight down to the sea below.   Truly breathtaking views of Mount Conero and the dramatic, rugged coast, with its jagged rocky formations can be enjoyed from this point as well as from any of the guestrooms.   The hotel itself is rather stark and modern with interiors softened by wicker couches topped by plump, yellow floral-print pillows, paintings and flower bouquets.   This is a summer resort with swimming pool and tennis available on the premises.   The all-white rooms are basic but comfortable with wicker and rattan beds and clean, tiled bathrooms.   The cuisine, friendly hospitality, and unforgettable panoramas compensate for the somewhat spartan decor.   *Directions:* Exit at Ancona Sud off autostrada A14 and follow signs for Camerano, then Portonuovo.   Watch for signs indicating the entrance to the hotel.

HOTEL EMILIA
Hosts: Fiorini Dubbini family
Portonuovo (AN) 60020, Italy
tel: (071) 801117 fax: (071) 801330
28 rooms with private bathrooms
Lire 100,000 double B&B
All meals served
Credit cards: all major
Open Easter-October
Some English spoken
Region: Marches

For those travelers wishing to explore the lesser-known Marches region or about to embark on a ferry to Greece or Yugoslavia, the unique Fortino hotel offers comfortable and relaxing accommodations.   Five km along the coast from the city of Ancona, the hotel boasts a beachfront location.   Originally a fortress, the vantage point it affords must have been viewed as strategic by Napoleon in 1811, when he ordered it to be constructed.   Fifteen guestrooms, three suites and a restaurant are housed within the low white, stone structure.   The restaurant specializes in fresh seafood dishes and looks so directly out to sea as to give the impression of being on a ship.   At the heart of the fort is a courtyard, complete with canons, where breakfast is served, and a separate building contains a bar and a spacious living room with fireplace, decorated in neoclassic style.   Rich period antiques appoint the three lovely suites, while simpler wicker furniture is found in the double rooms.   Just two steps away is the beach, and up on the roof of the one-story fort is a deck with a spectacular coastal view.   *Directions:* From Ancona, follow signs for Camerano.   Take a left at Portonuovo, heading down to the sea. Watch for signs indicating the hotel's entrance.

FORTINO NAPOLEONICO
Hosts:The Roscioni family
Portonuovo (AN) 60020, Italy
tel: (071) 801125 fax: (071) 801314
15 rooms and 3 suites with private bathrooms
Lire 165,000 double B&B
All meals served
Credit cards: all major
Open Easter-October
English spoken well
Region: Marches

Accommodation of all levels is available in Positano's many hotels: from five-star luxury to simple bed and breakfasts.   Casa Cosenza, with its sunny yellow facade, fits into the latter category.   Sitting snug against the cliffside, halfway down to the beach, it is reached by descending one of the variety of stairways found in this unique seaside town.   The front arched entranceway, lined with terracotta pots overflowing with colorful local flora, leads to an enormous tiled terrace overlooking the pastel-color houses of Positano and the dramatic coastline.   Seven guestrooms on the second floor, each with private bathroom, enjoy the same breathtaking panorama.   The residence dates back 200 years, as evidenced by the typical cupola ceilings in each room, originally designed to keep rooms cool and airy.   Rooms have bright, tiled floors and are simply and sweetly decorated with old-fashioned armoires, desks and beds.   Room #7, although with an older bathroom, has a lovely large terrace.   The helpful and very friendly Cosenza family assures visitors a pleasant stay.   *Directions:* It is best to leave your car in town and ask for directions, as it is impossible to indicate which stairway to take.

CASA COSENZA
Hosts: The Cosenza family
Positano (SA) 84017, Italy
tel: (089) 875063
7 rooms with private bathrooms
Lire 85,000 double
No meals served
Open Easter-October
No English spoken
Region: Campania

The spectacular Amalfi Coast is a stranger to agritourism, nor is there a plethora of bed-and-breakfast-like accommodations, so the Fenice is a real find. The place is as fantastic as the mythological bird for which it is named. Guests leave their cars on the main road from Positano and climb the arbored steps to discover the idyllic white villa hidden amid the lush Mediterranean vegetation. The charming, young proprietors, Constantino and Angela Mandara welcome new arrivals on the shady front terrace, where each clement morning breakfast is served accompanied by classical music. Six spacious bedrooms, each with spotless bath and a terrace with seaviews that will leave you breathless are situated in one wing of the family's antique-filled home. Seven more rooms, reached down many steps from the road, are built into the side of the cliff and have colorful, tiled floors and simpler furnishings. Descending yet more steps (always surrounded by incredible coastal views), you'll come across the curved seawater pool and jacuzzi carved against the rock, where a fresh Mediterranean lunch is served at one big table, prepared primarily with ingredients grown on the premises. Constantino also attends to the olive-oil and wine production. This property is a natural wonder, falling down to the sea and a small private beach. *Directions:* Located on the coastal highway south of Positano in the direction of Amalfi.

LA FENICE
Hosts: Constantino & Angela Mandara
Via Marconi 4
Positano (SA) 84017, Italy
tel: (089) 875513
13 rooms with private bathrooms
Lire 130,000 double B&B
Breakfast and lunch served
Open all year
Very little English spoken
Region: Campania

　　　　　Places to Stay

The Fattoria di Canneto rates high among Italian bed and breakfasts, due to its setting, style and charming proprietors, the noble Rucellai family. From the moment you enter the grand foyer looking out over the classical Italian renaissance garden of this 16th-century country villa, all sense of time and place is lost. The Rucellai's devotion to their "farm" (in the family since 1765) is apparent, as is their warm and enthusiastic hospitality. Guests are given the run of the charming old home: from the cozy bedrooms, antique-filled library and spacious living room with fireplace, plump floral sofas and family portraits to the country kitchen and breakfast room overlooking a 14th-century pool, where guests are served *en famille* at a long wooden table. Counting grandchildren, the family has 12 members, with the eldest daughter, Isabelle, being responsible for organizing itineraries and cultural events such as art courses, concerts and art exhibits. The Fattoria Canneto provides truly special accommodation as well as serving as an excellent base from which to visit Florence (30 km), Siena (90 km), Lucca and Pisa. *Directions:* From Florence take the A11 autostrada, exiting at Prato Est. Turn right on Viale della Repubblica, then left on Borgo Valsugana which leads up to the villa overlooking the city of Prato, long known for textile manufacturing.

FATTORIA DI CANNETO
Hosts: Countess & Count Rucellai
Via di Canneto 16
Prato (FI) 50047, Italy
tel: (0574) 460392/467748
24 rooms, 6 with private bathrooms
Lire 75,000 double B&B
Breakfast only
Open all year
Fluent English spoken
Region: Tuscany

One option (among at least 20 possibilities) for in-home accommodations in the Radda area is at the home of a gregarious Florentine couple, Giuliana and Enis Vergelli. On a long, winding road just before the castle/village of Volpaia is their stone house. The guest quarters are actually found in another stone house a few steps away in the quaint 14th-century village. The wood-shuttered residence can be rented entirely or as two separate apartments. One apartment is just like a dollhouse, comprised of a mini living area with minuscule fireplace, kitchenette and a ladder staircase leading up to the bedroom and bath; an absolutely adorable love nest for two. The other apartment, also on two floors, has a good-size living room with kitchen, bathroom and two bedrooms, simply and very comfortably furnished. Guests are welcome to wander through the Vergelli's garden and enjoy the terrace with sweeping views over Chianti country. Giuliana adores pampering her guests and appears now and then with jams, honey or a freshly made soup. *Directions:* Driving through the town of Radda, turn right at signs for Volpaia castle. Follow uphill for several km to the first house before entering town, marked Vergelli.

AZIENDA AGRICOLA VERGELLI
Hosts: Enis & Giuliana Vergelli
Localita: Volpaia
Radda in Chianti (SI) 53017, Italy
tel: (0577) 738382
2 apartments
Lire 450,000 weekly for 2 people
550,000 weekly for 4 people
No meals served
Open all year
No English spoken
Region: Tuscany

Positioned atop a hill in the very heart of the Chianti region, sits Castelvecchi, a stone village rich in history dating back to the Middle Ages. Son Giovanni Catania runs the family's wine estate there with great vivacity and the pride that comes with cultivating land that has been in his family for 300 years. Today the estate is completely and faithfully restored. The eight double rooms are located in the 18th-century villa, while the five apartments (available for weekly stays) are found in surrounding stone buildings, originally dwellings for the farm hands. The rooms, each given the name of a native flower, are complete with all amenities, new bathrooms, good antique reproductions, wrought-iron beds and ornate chandeliers. A continental breakfast (or full upon request) is served in a large, bright room with terrace. A round swimming pool and extensive garden make up the front yard of the villa, and offer an enticing spot to relax. This is an excellent base to explore the many captivating corners of Chianti and learn more about the hundreds of varieties of this famous wine. *Directions:* Castelvecchi is exactly halfway between Florence and Siena. From Siena follow signs for Castellina in Chianti, then Radda. Castelvecchi is just north of town and is well-marked. From Florence, either take the Chianti road (longer but extremely scenic) to Greve, Panzano and Castelvecchi; or take Tavernelle exit from the Florence-Siena superstrada.

FATTORIA CASTELVECCHI
Hosts: Catania family
Radda in Chianti (SI) 53017, Italy
tel: (0577) 738050 fax: (0577) 738608
8 rooms with private bathrooms, 5 apartments
Lire 92,000 double B&B
Breakfast only
Open all year
English spoken well
Region: Tuscany

For its combination of idyllic location, charming ambience and delightful hosts, the Podere Terreno is an example of the best of Italian bed and breakfasts. Sylvie and Roberto, a Franco-Italian couple, dedicate their lives to pampering their guests and seem to get as much enjoyment out of it as their guests do. The 400-year-old house is surrounded by terracotta flower vases, a grapevine-covered pergola for lounging, a small lake for dips, and sweeping panoramas of the Chianti countryside. Within are seven sweet double bedrooms with bath, each decorated differently with country antiques and the family's personal possessions; a wine cellar loaded with the proprietors' own Chianti Classico; and a billiard room/library. However, the highlight of a stay here is what awaits you after an arduous day of sightseeing. Guests first convene in the main room of the house around the massive stone fireplace on fluffy floral sofas for hors d'oeuvres and conversation, before sitting down to a sumptuous candelit dinner. Prepared completely by your hosts, the meal is served at an impeccably-set long wooden table. Between courses, one's eye naturally wanders about the cozy, stone-walled room, filled with country antiques, brass pots and dried flower bouquets hanging from the exposed beams, and shelves lined with bottles of wine. Absolutely delightful. *Directions:* Leaving Radda, follow signs for road to Volpaia. After 5 km, turn right at sign for Podere Terreno.

PODERE TERRENO
Hosts: Sylvie Haniez & Roberto Melosi
Via della Volpaia
Radda in Chianti (SI) 53017, Italy
tel: (0577) 738312
7 rooms with private bathrooms
Lire 95,000 per person half board
Breakfast and dinner served
Open all year
English spoken very well
Region: Tuscany

Both Radda and Greve are excellent bases from which to explore scenic chianti wine country with its regal castles and stone villages, plus Siena, Florence and San Gimignano. Radda in particular offers a myriad of possibilities for accommodation, including private homes whose owners have coordinated a booking service so that if space is not available at one, similar arrangements can be made elsewhere. The Val delle Corti is the home and vineyard estate of the ex-mayor of Radda, Giorgio Bianchi (who runs the booking service) and his lovely wife, Elli. The cozy pale-stone house with white shutters tops a hill overlooking town. The hosts, who moved here 20 years ago from Milan, are extremely active in community affairs and are a superb source for area information. They offer guests a quarter of their home: a comfortable two-bedroom apartment with a separate entrance, a large bathroom, kitchen with all necessities, and living room with fireplace, all furnished simply with family belongings. Upon request, Ella will supply coffee and jam for the weekly stay, while others meals can be taken at their nephew's newly opened restaurant in town, Le Vigne. *Directions:* Equidistant from Florence and Siena off the N222 Chianti road. Before entering Radda, turn right toward San Sano, then take first left at Val delle Corti.

PODERE VAL DELLE CORTI
Hosts: Giorgio & Elli Bianchi
Localita: La Croce
Radda in Chianti (SI) 53017, Italy
tel: (0577) 738215
1 apartment
Lire 500,000 per week
Half-board available at Le Vigne restaurant
Open Easter-November
English spoken very well
Region: Tuscany

On the opposite side of town from the Podere Val delle Corti (see preceding page), live Giorgio Bianchi's sister and family, who offer a two-bedroom apartment in a stone tower dating from 1832. This unique accommodation, perfect for a family of four, has an enchanting view of Radda and the countryside. The three-story tower has wood floors and beamed ceilings, a living room/kitchenette on the ground floor, one bedroom and a bath on the second floor, and a second bedroom on top. Furnishings are simple and in keeping with tower's rustic features. A small olive grove separates the tower from the Vitali's lovely home, where a swimming pool awaits road-weary guests. Lele is a vivacious hostess who divides her time between guests; a small in-house weaving business; and helping out her son and daughter-in-law, a young and ambitious couple who converted a farmhouse into the most authentic regional restaurant in town (Le Vigne). A half-board meal plan can be arranged for guests of the tower. *Directions:* From either Siena or Florence, follow signs for Radda off the spectacular "Strada del Chianti" N222. Go through town until you reach the hotel/restaurant Villa Miranda (*not* recommended), after which turn right at sign for Canvalle and follow dirt road up to the tower.

TORRE CANVALLE
Hosts: General & Lele Bianchi Vitali
Localita: La Villa
Radda in Chianti (SI) 53017, Italy
tel: (0577) 738321
1 apartment
Lire 550,000 weekly
Half board available at Le Vigne restaurant
Open Easter-November
English spoken very well
Region: Tuscany

Located in the far right-hand corner of the Chianti region is the Cortille farm, lovingly run by Florentine native Irene Gargani and her daughter's family. From its hilltop vantage point, the 16th-century, rustic stone farmhouse enjoys sweeping panoramic views of the countryside; as far as Siena on one side, and overlooking the picture-perfect stone village of Rapale on the other. The Gargani's wine production provides their primary livelihood. Three guestrooms, each with its own private bath, are located upstairs in the farmhouse, alongside the family quarters. The ambience is very cozy and nostalgic, the rooms nicely cluttered with what may well be grandmother's antique country furniture, family photographs, lace curtains and portrait paintings. Guests dine together either in the beamed dining room with hanging brass pots or out on the cypress-lined patio overlooking the valley. Bordering Umbria, the Cortille is situated just an hour from Florence and equidistant to Siena, Arezzo, Cortona, Lago Trasimeno and Chianti. Its location makes it an ideal, and homey, base from which to readily explore these cultural treasures. *Directions:* From the A1 highway between Firenze-Arezzo, take the Valdarno exit. Follow signs for Montevarchi and Bucine, then take a left up to Rapale.

FATTORIA CORTILLE
Hosts: Irene Gargani & family
Localita: Rapale
Bucine (AR) 52021, Italy
tel: (055) 998000
3 rooms with private bathrooms
Lire 55,000 per person half board
Breakfast and dinner served
Open all year
English spoken well
Region: Tuscany

The Amalfi Coast has always been a favorite seaside escape for Italians and Americans (especially honeymooners), and Positano and Ravello are the cream of the resort areas. The best accommodations in Ravello are described in *Italian Country Inns & Itineraries*, however, the Villa Amore, a small family-run hotel is an economical alternative. It is five minutes by foot from the main square in the direction of the romantic gardens of Villa Cimbrone. (Also not to be missed are the gardens of Villa Rufolo.) A stone-walled path takes you to the simple hotel where a flight of stairs leads to the reception and sitting areas and the veranda restaurant surrounded by a flower garden. Here, high above the sea, guests are treated to one of the coast's more spectacular views. Several of the twelve rooms that friendly hostess, Ermerinda, offers, open out to this same garden with its potted geraniums and lounge chairs. Rooms with baths are rather basic, but are pleasant and clean. Local savory specialties, many of them seafood-based, are served either inside or out on the terrace looking down to the turquoise sea. *Directions:* From the square follow signs for Villa Cimbone, watching for Villa Amore, which is on the way.

VILLA AMORE
Host: Ermerinda Schiavo
Ravello (SA) 84010, Italy
tel: (089) 857135
12 rooms with private bathrooms
Lire 85,000 double B&B
All meals served
Open Easter-October
Little English spoken
Region: Campania

The Villa Maria is perhaps best known for its absolutely delightful terrace restaurant which has a bird's-eye view of the magnificent coast. Whereas most of Ravello's hotels capture the southern view, the Villa Maria features the equally lovely vista to the north. The Villa Maria is located two minutes by foot from the main square on the path winding to the Villa Cimbrone. After parking in the square (or at the Hotel Giordano), look for signs for the Villa Maria, which you'll find perched on the cliffs to your right. The building is a romantic old villa with a garden stretching to the side where tables and chairs are set, a favorite place to dine while enjoying the superb view. Inside, there is a cozy dining room overlooking the garden. The bedrooms are furnished with antique pieces including brass beds. The bathrooms have been freshly remodeled and some even have jacuzzi tubs. The hotel is owned by Vincenzo Palumbo whose staff speaks excellent English. Vincenzo also owns the nearby Hotel Giordano where there is a heated pool that you can use. You can expect and warm and gracious welcome at the Villa Maria, where guests are lucky enough to have the best of all worlds: a wonderful view and location in a charming villa with a fine restaurant. *Directions:* Ravello is about 6 km north of Amalfi on a small road heading north from highway 163.

VILLA MARIA
Host: Vincenzo Palumbo
Via San Chiara 2
84010 Ravello (SA) 84010, Italy
tel: (089) 857255 fax: (089) 857071
12 rooms with private bathrooms
Lire 120,000-140,000 double B&B
All meals served
Credit cards: all major
Open all year
English spoken very well
Region: Campania

In the foothills of the Dolomites 90 km north of Venice on the autostrada, is an historical town called Vittorio Veneto. The surrounding countryside is entrancing and the lifestyle tranquil, so it is no wonder that after having seen a good part of the world, Aldo and Matilde Bach settled here with their five children and opened a bed and breakfast. The attractive rust-color farmhouse overlooks their own orchards and vineyards lining soft green hills, with dramatic snowcapped peaks in the distance. Practicing what they believe to be the true spirit of agritourism, guests are given fresh linens (no towels) and are responsible for making their own beds and tidying their rooms. The nine rustic rooms with individual bathrooms are spotless and comfortable. There is also one two-bedroom apartment with living room and kitchenette. Guests convene at mealtime around a big table in the cozy dining quarters for local delicacies prepared by our enthusiastic and personable hosts using fresh and organically grown produce and no fats. The many comments of gratitude written in the guest book are proof of a memorable stay. *Directions:* From the A27 highway, exit at Vittorio Veneto/Revine Lago and follow yellow signs up to Le Selve.

FATTORIA LE SELVE
Hosts: Aldo & Matilde Bach
Via Lame 26
Revine Lago (TV) 31020, Italy
tel: (0438) 583515 or (041) 5287604
9 rooms, several with private bathrooms, 1 apartment
Lire 50,000 per person half board only
  3-day minimum stay
Breakfast and dinner served
Open Easter-October
Fluent English spoken
Region: Veneto

Tuscany is the most visited region in Italy--mostly between Siena and Florence--but it nonetheless contains many other treasures off the beaten track. Heading west from Florence toward the coast are the lovely towns of Lucca and Pisa, and just north of them is the beautifully scenic area known as Garfagnana, which features two nature reserves and the Apuan Alps. Here in the northernmost tip of Tuscany is evidence of how Italian culture varies not only from one region to another, but within a region itself. In the heart of these mountains, the genial Coletti family has been running a lively restaurant and cultivating cereals, wild berries and chestnuts. Just recently, the Colettis have added a B&B to their list of activities. Seven double rooms with a mountain-cabin feeling, pinewood floors and ceilings, have been fashioned in a restored three-story building in the stone village of Roggio. Most have a balcony and all have very nice modern bathrooms. Meals are taken around the corner at the family restaurant where Gemma Coletti prepares her special lasagna and polenta with porcini mushrooms, among other local specialties. *Directions:* From Lucca, take route 445 toward Castelnuovo and on to Roggio. Take a left up a winding road to Roggio, where a sign indicates the Da Gemma restaurant in the village.

AZIENDA COLETTI
Hosts: Gemma & Severino Coletti
Localita: Vagli Sotto
Roggio (LU) 55100, Italy
tel: (0583) 649179
7 rooms with private bathrooms
Lire 40,000 double B&B
All meals served
Open all year
Some English spoken
Region: Tuscany

The Hotel Cesari, just off the busy Via del Corso in the heart of the city, is a reputable hotel with a long-standing tradition of hospitality. The Cesari opened its doors over 200 years ago (in 1787) and has numbered among its guests such illustrious individuals as Stendhal, Garibaldi and Mazzini. The hotel maintains a pleasant, old-world flavor, if slightly worn around the edges. However, the fact that the establishment has not been recently renovated is reflected in the relatively low room rates charged by the proprietors, which make it a good value in an expensive city. A double salon decorated with plump red-leather armchairs, worn oriental carpets, period paintings and ornate chandeliers greets arriving visitors. The spacious guestrooms all include a private bath, and are simple and comfortable, with soft floral armchairs and older furnishings. Breakfast is served in the rooms, as there is no common dining area. The hotel staff were exceptionally courteous and helpful. *Directions:* Use a detailed city map to locate the hotel off the Via del Corso.

HOTEL CESARI
Host: Anna Palumbo
Via di Pietra 89
01186 Rome, Italy
tel: (06) 6792386 fax: (06) 6790882
45 rooms with private bathrooms
Lire 140,000 double B&B
Breakfast only
Credit cards: VS
Open all year
English spoken well
Region: Lazio

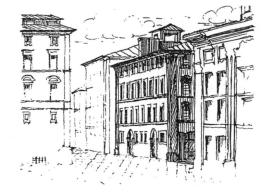

The Due Torri is a perfect example of a small and charming city hotel, a breed not easy to find in today's urban centers.   The building, dating to the early 1800s, is tucked away on a tiny, narrow street in the quiet historical section of Rome between the Spanish Steps and Navona Square.   Freshly renovated one year ago, the twenty six small bedrooms are decorated with care and taste and feature spotless bathrooms, period antiques and peach-colored fabric walls.   Many amenities are offered, including elevator and air conditioning, which provides welcome (if not critical) relief on hot Roman summer days.   The cozy and impressive reception, sitting area and breakfast room have oriental carpets, cream draperies, gilt-framed mirrors and paintings, and elegant tapestry chairs.   A rooftop terrace currently is being restored, and is scheduled for use by the end of this year.   The very friendly staff is eager to make suggestions for local sightseeing. The superbly located Due Torri is a popular hotel, so be sure to reserve your room at least one month in advance.   *Directions:* Use a detailed city map to locate the hotel, north of Navona square amidst a maze of winding streets.

HOTEL DUE TORRI
Host: Cesare Picozza
Vicolo del Leonetto 23
00186 Rome, Italy
tel: (06) 6876983 fax: (06) 6875765
26 rooms with private bathrooms
Lire 180,000 double B&B
Breakfast only
Credit cards: AX VS
Open all year
English spoken well
Region: Lazio

Many hotels in Rome can boast panoramic views over the city, but few have such a close up view of a world-famous monument as the delightful Fontana Hotel. Situated directly on the square containing the beautiful Trevi fountain, the Fontana's windows look out on to its gushing waters, into which you can practically toss a coin from your room. The fountain has only recently been brought back to life following years of tedious restoration work, and is magnificent. The sleek black-and-white breakfast room doubles as a bar and is situated on the top floor of the 17th-century building, giving guests a bird's-eye view over the square from an enormous picture window. The twenty seven rooms are sweetly done with pastel-floral wallpaper, white curtains and bedspreads, and immaculate bathrooms. Vaulted ceilings crown the narrow halls leading to the guestrooms, and are adorned with antique prints of Rome. Signor Mario and Signora Elena at the desk handily attend to guests' every need. The noise commonly associated with a city hotel is not a problem here as the square is closed to traffic, and the fountain closes at midnight. *Directions:* Use a detailed city map to locate hotel in the Piazza di Trevi off the Via Tritone.

FONTANA HOTEL
Host: Dottore Gazzabin
Piazza di Trevi 96
00187 Rome, Italy
tel: (06) 6786113/6791056
27 rooms with private bathrooms
Lire 181,000 double B&B
Breakfast only
Credit cards: VS
Open all year
English spoken well
Region: Lazio

The Locarno Hotel is a wonderful option in the urban B&B category. Centrally located on the corner of a rather busy street, it is only two blocks from bustling Popolo Square. Its downtown location makes noise unavoidable, so it is advisable to request a room which is not over the street. The palazzo housing the Locarno dates back to the turn of the century, and the hotel itself opened in 1925. Even with the extensive renovations it has undergone, the establishment retains the art-deco flavor it had originally. The red-carpeted reception area leads to a cozy bar and long mirrored sitting room lined with cushioned banquettes and cafe tables where breakfast is served. There is also a side patio with shady canvas umbrellas where guests can take breakfast in warm weather. (A rooftop terrace and larger breakfast room are currently under construction.) The twenty two double rooms with bathrooms are decorated with antiques, gold-framed mirrors and pretty floral wallpaper. The Locarno features such extras as a parking garage and free use of bright red bicycles with which you might tour the Villa Borghese park. It is no wonder that this is a favorite among artists and writers. Reserve well in advance. *Directions:* Use detailed city map to locate hotel one block east of the Tiber River at Flaminia square sign.

HOTEL LOCARNO
Host: Maria Teresa Celli
Via della Penna 22
00186 Rome, Italy
tel: (06) 3610841 fax: (06) 3215249
22 rooms and 2 suites with private bathrooms
Lire 193,000 double B&B
Breakfast only
Credit cards: AX VS
Open all year
English spoken well
Region: Lazio

This small centrally located hotel gets its name, as you might guess, along with its relatively high prices, from its proximity to Rome's most famous square just three blocks away. The hotel has been in business since the 1920s and has been just recently renovated. The contained, mirrored reception and sitting area is divided by a sweeping red-carpeted stairway leading up to the twenty guestrooms found on three floors. The rooms are neat and clean, if somewhat uninspired, and feature private baths and simple, practical furnishings. The top-floor rooms also have small balconies lined with flowerpots. Breakfast can be arranged and served in rooms upon request, but it is not included in double rate. The cordial owners, Signor and Signora Giocondi, have been operating the hotel for the past 30 years, and are always present and happy to answer any questions. The hotel's location means guests are within easy walking distance of excellent restaurants and some of the most famous boutiques in the world. *Directions:* Use a detailed city map to locate hotel three blocks west of the Piazza di Spagna.

HOTEL PIAZZA DI SPAGNA
Owner: Signori Giocondi
Via Mario di Fiori 61
00187 Rome, Italy
tel: (06) 6796412 fax: (06) 6790654
24 rooms with private bathrooms
Lire 180,000 double
No meals served
Credit cards: VS
Open all year
Very little English spoken
Region: Lazio

Just north of the famous Navona Square with its marvelous Bernini fountains is the small and centrally located Portoghesi Hotel in the oldest section of Rome. A landmark hotel, accommodation has been offered here for over 150 years, and every effort has been made to maintain an intimate, family-run atmosphere. The property was recently given a facelift, and now most rooms have new, private bathrooms plus air conditioning, telephone and TV. An elevator takes guests up to the guestrooms, which are decorated in two distinct styles: a clean and simple modern look or, as with the preferred corner rooms #8, #24 and #44, simple and elegant with antique beds and armoires. Each floor has its own cozy sitting area with gilded mirrors, paintings and antique chairs. A pleasant extra is the rooftop terrace overlooking the terracotta roofs typical of Rome, as well as the cupola of the famous church after which the hotel and street are named. Breakfast is served on this arbored, outdoor terrace in the warmer months. Reserve at least one month in advance. Signor Mario and his sons attentively look after the needs of their guests. *Directions:* Use a detailed city map to locate the hotel in the heart of Rome.

HOTEL PORTOGHESI
Host: Mario Trivellone
Via dei Portoghesi 1
00186 Rome, Italy
tel: (06) 6864231 fax: ((06) 6876976
26 rooms with private bathrooms
Lire 150,000 double B&B
Breakfast only
Credit cards: VS
Open all year
English spoken well
Region: Lazio

The exceptionally priced Hotel Tea, just a few blocks from the internationally famous Via Veneto, lined with foreign embassies and chic boutiques, has been catering to embassy visitors for over 30 years. The turn-of-the-century building was originally the private residence of the Princess Tea until the Moioli family bought it in 1960. Signor Moioli's son has just recently returned to Rome from the United States with his American wife, Anne, who heartily welcomes guests at the front desk. Anne has enthusiastically tackled the task of giving the hotel a badly needed facelift. The thirty five rooms each have a distinct personality, combining as they do a variety of floral-print wallpaper, wrought-iron beds, small sofas (that can be used as a third bed) and worn oriental carpets. There is a warm and pleasantly homey feeling to the place once you've gotten past the rather dreary entrance. A favorite spot is the elegant high-ceiling living room with its pastel-blue fabric chairs, chandeliers, and enormous painted portrait, leftover from the days of Princess Tea. Downstairs is the tavern restaurant and two other living rooms where breakfast is served. Ask for a suite, which are priced the same as doubles. *Directions:* Use detailed city map to locate the hotel four blocks east of Via Veneto.

HOTEL TEA
Hosts: Giulio Moioli family
Via Sardegna 149
00187 Rome, Italy
tel: (06) 465964
35 rooms with private bathrooms
Lire 134,000 double B&B
Breakfast only
Credit cards: VS
Open all year
Fluent English spoken
Region: Lazio

The Teatro di Pompeo, a well-managed, efficient and friendly small hotel, gets its name from the ruins of the Pompeius Theater (55 BC) which were discovered within the foundation of the building. The pale yellow hotel is centrally located between Navona Square and Campo dei Fiori Square, an area characterized by authentic local color and narrow streets lined with artisan's workshops. It is fast becoming the place to live in the city, and every other building has been restored and painted in the wonderful, faded earth tones so typical of Rome. Signor Luigi at reception enthusiastically welcomes guests to the twelve new and spotless bedrooms, simply and tastefully decorated with antique prints of ancient Rome and warmed overhead by original beamed ceilings. Many amenities, including air conditioning (supplemental charge), spotless bathrooms, TV and telephone are available in each room. Descending a short flight of stairs from the mini-reception and bar area brings you to the dark, cave-like breakfast room, unique in that it is part of the ancient theater. Next door is the Pallaro restaurant, a favorite with the local citizenry, where guests can treat themselves to a genuine Roman meal. *Directions:* Use a detailed city map to locate hotel three blocks east of Campo dei Fiori square.

HOTEL TEATRO DI POMPEO
Host: Lorenzo Mingnone
Largo del Pallaro 8
01186 Rome, Italy
tel: (06) 6872812   fax: (06) 6544431
12 rooms with private bathrooms
Credit cards: VS
Lire 190,000 double B&B
Breakfast only
Open all year
English spoken well
Region: Lazio

Behind the city gates of Porta Pinciana, whose ancient walls lead from the Via Veneto, is tranquil, tree-lined Via Nomentana, once a luxurious residential street in this part of the city.　Many elegant pastel-colored villas remain (including that of Mussolini), but the majority of them have been converted into embassy-owned apartments over the years.　The Villa del Parco has been transformed into a lovely and quiet hotel with a B&B feel to it.　A flower-edged driveway leads to the villa, passing tables set up for breakfast in the small front garden.　The sensation upon entering the pleasant lobby scattered with antiques is that you've arrived home. Two cozy sitting rooms invite guests to sit and relax.　The twenty guestrooms, each with private bath, are divided among the three floors of the hotel.　Half of the bedrooms have been renovated and they all vary greatly in size and decor, which tends to be a mixture of old and new furnishings.　Request one of the newer rooms facing out the back of the hotel just in case of street noise.　The Bartolini family is happy to make restaurant suggestions and, as parking is always a problem, take note that a reputable garage (with limousine service) is located across the street. *Directions:* Rely on a detailed city map to locate the hotel in a residential district a 15 minute walk from the center of town.

HOTEL VILLA DEL PARCO
Hosts: Bartolini family
Via Nomentana 110
Rome 00161, Italy
tel: (06) 864115
20 rooms with private bathrooms
Lire 185,000 double B&B
Breakfast only
Credit cards: all major
Open all year
Some English spoken
Region: Lazio

Every place in Italy seems to be famous for some type of food or wine, and Parma is no exception, being without doubt the city most internationally known for its cheese and prosciutto, which you should not fail to sample while you're in the region. Thirty km from Parma are found the curative thermal waters of Salsomaggiore and, just beyond town is the Antica Torre. The ancient 13th-century tower majestically crowns a hilltop overlooking the soft green countryside. The Pavesi family, proprietors of the surrounding farm, offer warm hospitality to its guests within the tower. One bedroom with bath is located on each of the tower's three floors and, in addition, the family has a large two-bedroom apartment available in the main house, which would be ideal for a family. Rooms are simply decorated, and have lovely views over the valley. There is also a swimming pool and horseback riding. The barn has been converted into a pleasant dining room where fortunate guests sit down together to a hearty homemade meal, typically Emiliana, including fresh pastas, vegetables, meat and poultry directly from the farm. *Directions:* From Salsomaggiore, go through town, following signs for Cangelasio and Antica Torre.

ANTICA TORRE
Hosts: Francesco Pavesi family
Localita: Cangelasio
Salsomaggiore Terme (PR) 43030, Italy
tel: (0524) 575425
3 rooms with private bathrooms, 1 apartment
Lire 80,000 double B&B
*   55,000 per person half board*
All meals served
Open all year
No English spoken
Region: Emilia-Romagna

Though near both Verona and Lake Garda, the Ca'Verde farm feels miles away from civilization, immersed in a wooded valley in the Veneto wine country. Nine families got together 12 years ago to purchase the unusual stone Provence-style farmhouse, originally a 15th-century convent, and have made it into a busy dairy farm. Their idea was to save the historic building, the many acres of land around it, and create local employment by producing cheese and yogurt on the farm. They adhere to traditional production methods without additives or preservatives. Five attic rooms have been fashioned for guests in the enormous U-shaped house where three of the families live. Rooms are small and utilitarian, with rustic wood beds, beamed ceilings with skylights and one clean, modern bathroom for every two rooms. A main attraction is the trattoria specializing in regional recipes (fresh pasta and truffles, vegetarian dishes) and homemade wine, served in three informal dining rooms with red-checked tablecloths and large fireplaces. Guests dine in or out on the patio, and in the summer are treated to outdoor concerts and cinema. *Directions:* From Verona take the A12 autostrada toward Brennero. Exit at Verona Nord, and follow signs for San Ambrogio. Go through town and start up hill, watching for small sign for Ca'Verde on left hand side of road.

CA'VERDE
Host: Alessandro Lanza
Azienda Agricola 8 Marzo
San Ambrogio Valpolicella (VR) 37020, Italy
tel: (045) 7730760
6 rooms sharing 2 bathrooms
Lire 42,000 double B&B
All meals served
Open March-November
Some English spoken
Region: Veneto

Due to the ever-increasing popularity of the stunning medieval village of San Gimignano, accommodations in the surrounding countryside have flourished. La Casanova is a typical square stone farmhouse with wood shutters and red-tile roof, which you'll grow accustomed to seeing throughout Tuscany. The bed and breakfast's exceptional feature is that it enjoys a privileged view of the towers of San Gimignano, an ancient town referred to as the Manhattan of the year 1000. Marisa and Monica Cappellini are jovial hostesses who pride themselves on offering comfortable and immaculate accommodations to their international clientele. Breakfast is served on the outside patio where guests are immersed in breathtaking scenery first thing in the morning before heading out to visit intriguing San Gimignano and the many surrounding villages. This is an authentic and simple wine-producing farm with eight double rooms with private baths. Country furniture characteristic of the region decorates the rooms, whose original architectural features have been preserved. *Directions:* From San Gimignano take the road toward Volterra. After 5 km, turn right at the sign for Casanova, *not* Hotel, Pescille.

CASANOVA DI PESCILLE
Host: Marisa Cappellini
Localita: Pescille
San Gimignano (SI) 53037, Italy
tel: (0577) 941902
8 doubles with private bathrooms
Lire 70,000 double B&B
Breakfast only
Open all year
No English spoken (some French)
Region: Tuscany

Accidentally coming upon the Casolare, tucked away in the hills five miles beyond medieval San Gimignano, was a delightful surprise.   Just before reaching the B&B, you'll see an abandoned stone convent dating back to 1100, causing the visitor's imagination to wander to the past.   Leaving the convent and the tourists behind, guests arriving at the Casolare feel like they're coming home.   The attractive renovated farmhouse, hosted by Andrea, a young antique dealer, retains all of the features characteristic of the original structure.   The four double rooms with bath are extremely comfortable and reflect superb taste.   The one suite and the common sitting room and dining room have been decorated with refined antiques as well.   Guests receive a folder of watercolor prints by a local artist depicting the various sites in the area with a description of each on the back.   The originals adorn an entire wall of the living room.   An extra bonus is the lovely pool which provides refreshment and relaxation after a hot day sightseeing, while anticipating another appetizing meal at dusk.   This is a truly tranquil spot. *Directions:* From San Gimignano follow signs for Montaione.   Staying right at the fork, turn right onto dirt road for Libbiano.

CASOLARE DI LIBBIANO
Host: Andrea Bucciarelli
Localita: Libbiano
San Gimignano (SI) 53037, Italy
tel: (0577) 955102
4 rooms and 1 suite with private bathrooms
Lire 80,000 per person half board
  3-day minimum stay
Breakfast and dinner served
Open Easter-October
Some English spoken
Region: Tuscany

The increasing popularity of this perfectly intact medieval town and the resulting availability of accommodations has made San Gimignano a hub from which tourists fan out to visit nearby, less-well-known treasures such as Volterra, Colle Val d'Elsa and Monteriggioni. A very pleasant stay can be experienced at the Podere Villuzza, run by friendly young Sandra and Gianni Dei. Following restoration of their 150-year-old stone farmhouse, two years ago they opened the doors to guests. Chairs are set up out in front where visitors can enjoy the view of vineyard-covered hills that lead up to the famous multi-towered town. A hearty dinner can be shared with other guests in the simple country-style dining room where Sandra prepares tantalizing, fresh specialties from the family recipe book. Her husband occupies himself with the production of top-quality Vernaccia wine. Two double rooms with nice new bathrooms are upstairs, furnished with wrought-iron beds and antique armoires, complemented by mansard ceilings. The larger double has a private terrace overlooking the back hills. Also available are three small apartments within the house which include a living area and kitchen. A two-year plan promises the addition of five rooms plus a restaurant for guests. *Directions:* Take the first right after town (gravel road). Follow signs for 2 km.

PODERE VILLUZZA
Hosts: Sandra & Gianni Dei
Strada 25
San Gimignano (SI) 53037, Italy
tel: (0577) 940585
2 rooms and 3 suites with private bathrooms
Lire 75,000 double B&B
Breakfast and dinner served
Open all year
Some English spoken
Region: Tuscany

In the heart of the wine valley of Piedmont, between the principal cities of Piedmont: Alessandria, Alba and Asti, is some lovely and serene countryside characterized by rolling green hills lined with vineyards and a strong tradition of fine country dining.   Maria and Piercarlo are a local couple who have dedicated their lives to their farm and its production of Barolo and Dolcetto wines, as did their parents and grandparents.   In fact, their typical white rectangular farmhouse has been in the family for well over 100 years.   Over those years, as the family grew, so did the main house, eventually being connected to the barn and stables to make room for everyone.   A family of just three, the Carellis found themselves with extra space and decided to use two of the bedrooms for guests, leaving grandmother's simple antiques in them, and adding one spotless bathroom in between them.   The dining room is popular with locals, and will serve up an unforgettable meal of homemade tagliatelle, lamb and other regional specialties. *Directions:* From San Marzano, take the road leading north from town toward Agliano, turning right at chapel and follow signs for the farm.

ANTICA FATTORIA DEL COLLE
Hosts: Maria & Piercarlo Carelli
Reg. Chierina 17
San Marzano Oliveto (AT) 14050, Italy
tel: (0141) 856252
2 rooms sharing 1 bathroom
Lire 40,000 per person half board
Breakfast and dinner served
Open all year
No English spoken
Region: Piedmont

On the other side of town from the Antica Fattoria (see previous page) is another typical farmhouse and vineyard run cooperatively by several local families. Three simple and very neat bedrooms upstairs are available for guests, decorated with country furniture typical of the area. The three rooms share one nearby bathroom. The farm work seems to be evenly divided among these energetic families, whose members convene along with locals at lunch time in the spacious and rustic restaurant on the premises, where they can count on a hearty full-course meal prepared from the freshest possible ingredients directly off their land. This provides a convenient location from which to launch excursions to some of the delightful villages in the immediate vicinity, and, of course, to Alba and Asti, which should not be missed. You can also take shorter trips on horseback from nearby stables into the scenic surrounding countryside. Or, alternatively, the Italian riviera lies just an hour and a half away. *Directions:* Coming from the direction of Nizza Monferrato, take the middle road at the triple fork just before San Marzano. La Viranda is just up the road on the left.

LA VIRANDA
Host: Emanuele Giordano
Localita: Corte 64
San Marzano Oliveto (AT) 14050, Italy
tel: (0140) 856571
3 rooms sharing 1 bathroom
Lire 40,000 per person half board
All meals served
Closed August
Some English spoken
Region: Piedmont

The complex of stone houses known as Borgo Spante dates back to the 15th Century and has been in the same family since 1752.   Consisting of a main villa, connecting farmers' houses, chapel, barns, swimming pool and garden, it is isolated in 500-acres of woods and hills, yet only 10 miles from Orvieto and not far from Assisi, Todi and Perugia.   Daughter Claudia decided to move into the summer residence full time and run a B&B.   Guests stay in a combination of rooms and apartments in the former farmers' houses, left intact with their irregular sized rooms, sloping worn-brick floors and rustic country furnishings; very charming in its way.   Meals are served in the dining room with wood tables and fireplace.   This arrangement will change by the end of the year when a larger dining area currently being created in the old barn/stalls will be completed, along with additional accommodations.   Memorable evenings are spent out in the garden conversing with other guests or listening to an impromptu concert.   *Directions:* From the A1 autostrada exit at Orvieto and follow signs for Arezzo on route 101.   After 7 km turn right at Morrano and proceed for 18 km until the sign for Spante.

BORGO SPANTE
Host: Claudia Spatola
Localita: Ospedaletto
San Venanzo (TR) 05010, Italy
tel: (075) 8709134 or (06) 8546408
4 rooms sharing 2 bathrooms
*   7 suite-apartments*
Lire 75,000 per person half board
*   weekly or weekend stay required*
Breakfast and dinner served upon request
Open all year
Some English spoken
Region: Umbria

There is a beautiful piece of coastline on the Adriatic Sea just south of Ancona which differs dramatically from the more flat and uninteresting shoreline to the north and south where modern hotels and condos proliferate. The quaint stone village of Sirolo sits high above the water on a mountainside looking down to the beaches of the Riviera Conero. Delightful seafood restaurants dot the shore, where you might enjoy a plate of pasta with fresh clams while watching the tide come in. Isabella and Vittorio Fabiani decided several years ago to open a B&B in 14th-century Sirolo, and offer four guestrooms above their small restaurant with its outdoor tables. The bedrooms are simply furnished in old-fashioned style, and most have sea views. By spring, all of them will have individual bathrooms, as well. The young couple is full of ideas to improve the premises but, being a historical building (legend has it that St. Francis stayed overnight here), even simple renovations are often restricted. Not even the faded green shutters adorning the windows can be touched. Nonetheless, the place exudes a basic charm. Meals are created in true Marchigiano style; natives of the Marches are known for their skill in the preparation of seafood dishes (brodetto). *Directions:* The Rocco is located in the town of Sirolo, after Portonuovo.

LOCANDA ROCCO
Hosts: Isabella & Vittorio Fabiani
Via Torrione 1
Sirolo (AN) 60020, Italy
tel: (071) 936088
4 rooms sharing 2 bathrooms
Lire 55,000 per person half board
All meals served
Open all year
Some English spoken
Region: Marches

The stone tower of Bagnara, dating back nearly a thousand years is situated in the Upper Tiber Valley just 20 km north of Perugia, and not far from the major cultural centers of Umbria, Assisi, Gubbio and Citta del Castello. The independent tower is part of the vast tobacco farm of the Tremi family who reside in a luxurious villa just down the hill. Three fully equipped apartment-suites accommodating two to six people have been fashioned within the tower (available for weekly rental only). The quarters come complete with kitchenette and are nicely furnished in a refined country style with antiques, painted wrought-iron beds, and matching floral curtains and bedspreads. Original architectural features such as beamed ceilings, terracotta floors and arched stone doorways, lend authentic medieval ambience to a stay here, and given the sweeping views it commands over the valley, it's easy to understand why this spot was chosen for a watchtower. The backdrop consists of wooded hills dotted with grazing livestock and distant farmhouses. An excellent and unusual base for thorough exploration of the natural and man-made wonders of this rich region. *Directions:* From Perugia, exit at Ponte Pattoli from highway 45. Follow signs for Umbertide, turning left at the second road, *not* right for Solfagnano. The Tremi villa is the first on the left.

LA TORRE DI BAGNARA
Hosts: Tremi family
Solfagnano (PG) 06080, Italy
tel: (075) 604136
3 suite-apartments
Lire 700,000-1,200,000 weekly
No meals served
Open all year
English spoken well
Region: Umbria

Halfway between Florence and Siena in the heart of the Chianti region is the Sovigliano farm, recently restored by a handsome couple from Verona, Claudio Bicego and his wife, who delight in welcoming international visitors into their warm home.   Guests have an independent entrance to the five bedrooms (only two with private bath), each very much in keeping with the pure simplicity of this typical farmhouse. Exposed-beam ceilings and terracotta floors, antique beds and armoires and a bucolic views make time stand still here.   There is also a two-bedroom apartment within the house, decorated in similar style, with kitchen and dining area.   The upstairs living room, sparsely furnished with the family's elegant antiques, kitchen with country fireplace and surrounding garden are for everyone's use.   Signor Claudio is actively involved in the production of top Tuscan wines in conjunction with several other wine estates, and also coordinates with other area residents to organize lessons in language, history and culinary arts with local professors. *Directions:* From Siena, exit the superstrada at Poggibonsi; from Florence at Tavarnelle.   Follow signs for Tavarnelle and, once in town, turn off at Magliano where signs indicate a small road to Sovigliano.

PODERE SOVIGLIANO
Hosts: The Bicego family
Via Magliano 9
Tavarnelle Val di Pesa (FI) 50028, Italy
tel: (055) 8076217
5 rooms, 2 with private bathrooms
   1 apartment
Lire 80,000 double B&B
   minimum stay 2 days
Dinner upon request
Open all year
English spoken well
Region: Tuscany

The scenic countryside south of Padua is called the Colli Eugenei. The area is known for producing an excellent wine and guarantees to reward the traveler who wants to wander a bit off the beaten track. Signora Luciana has transformed her lovely cream-color 16th-century Venetian villa into a six-room bed and breakfast, with splendid results. Set in a tranquil green valley below the small hillside village of Teolo, the house is completely surrounded by a magnificent flower garden with roses, pansies, magnolias, forsythia and fruit trees--all in full bloom and a sight to behold in early spring. In the center of this lush little paradise is a swimming pool, a welcome source of refreshment for road-weary guests. There is an air of romance within the villa, elegantly appointed with period paintings, colorful floral-print sofas and armchairs, and a grand chandelier in the handsome foyer. The six guestrooms have individual baths, and are tastefully decorated with antique furnishings. Guests dine at separate tables in the gracious dining room. La Villa is affiliated with a nearby club and restaurant offering tennis and horseback-riding facilities. *Directions:* From Padova follow signs for Monte grotto Terme, then Teolo. Watch for driveway to La Villa on the left after passing through the center of town.

LA VILLA
Host: Signora Luciana Brunello
Via della Villa 6
Teolo (PD) 35037, Italy
tel: (049) 9902178
6 rooms with private bathrooms
Lire 70,000 per person half board
Breakfast and dinner served
Open March-December
English spoken well
Region: Veneto

You would never happen upon the Residenza San Andrea al Farinaio because it is located so far off the beaten path that you must write or call ahead for detailed instructions if you ever hope to find it. Once you have settled in, however, the location is quite convenient as a home base for exploring both Tuscany and Umbria. And, for those looking for well-priced accommodation without sacrificing comfort, this bed and breakfast might be the perfect selection. The oldest part of the inn dates back to the 13th century when it was home to the priests tending a church which stood across the road. The present owner, Patrizia Nappi, is a warm and gracious hostess, speaks excellent English and has lovingly transformed the old stone house into a cozy inn, combining modern pictures, furniture and knick-knacks with lovely antiques. Of the five bedrooms, three have private baths. A personal favorite is the large guest room at the top of the steps. The most wonderful area in the house is the dining room with its massive darken-wood beams, large open fireplace, beautiful antique trestle table, colorful plates adorning the walls and lots of copper pots and pans. If you make arrangements in advance, you can dine here with other guests, sharing a simple, superb meal family-style at the long, handsome candlelit table in front of a crackling fire. *Directions:* Head southeast from Cortona to Terontola (approximately 10 km).

RESIDENZA SAN ANDREA AL FARINAIO
Host: Patrizia Nappi
San Andrea al Farinaio, 118
Terontola di Cortona, (AR) 52040, Italy
tel: (0575) 677736
5 rooms, 3 with private bathrooms
Lire 130,000 double B&B
Breakfast and dinner served
Open all year
Fluent English spoken
Region: Umbria

Practically 70 percent of the families residing in the Alto Adige mountain region offer B&B accommodations so, unless it's Christmas or August, a bed is not hard to come by.   This is a region with a distinct Austrian flavor where more German than Italian is spoken, and where more wurstel than pasta is likely to be   served at the table.   The warm Trompedeller family heartily welcome international travelers to their typical Tyrolian-style home.   The six guestrooms each have a private bath, and are modestly decorated with basic light-wood furniture and accented with orange and brown curtains and bedspreads--a decor common to the B&B in this region.   The cozy wood-paneled dining room boasts a splendid panoramic view over the mountain cliffs and green foothills.   The house is located several miles outside the quaint town of Tiers on a road which comes to an end at a babbling brook surrounded by hushed woods with hiking trails.   Depending on the season, guests can take advantage of the Val Gardena ski slopes or summer mountain climbing.   *Directions:* From the Verona-Brennero autostrada, exit at Bolzano Nord and follow signs for Tiers.   Go through the town and make a hairpin left turn at the chapel.

VERALTENHOF
Hosts: Josef Trompedeller family
Oberstrasse 61
Tiers (BZ) 39050, Italy
tel: (0471) 642102
6 rooms with private bathrooms
Lire 35,000 per person half board
Breakfast and dinner served
Open all year
No English spoken
Region: Alto Adige

Since 1830, the 12th-century castle and 4,000-acre farm of Titignano has figured among the many properties of the noble Corsini family.   Five years ago the family decided to participate in the increasingly popular agriturismo trade by offering six guestrooms in the main house, with plans to add a swimming pool and 12 new apartments in the farmers quarters already under restoration.   The undertaking is primarily the responsibility of the Fontanis, a delightful young couple who take care of everything from looking after guests and the farm to cooking and serving. Meals are shared at a long table in one of the castle's graciously neglected rooms with an enormous gray stone fireplace sporting the family coat of arms, and lofty ceilings made of the stamped terracotta blocks typical of Umbria.   Off the dining hall are the spacious bedrooms, each with modernized pink travertine bathrooms and decorated eclectically with unrefined antiques and wrought-iron beds. Common areas include a living room with bright floral sofas around a fireplace, a game and TV room for children, and a large terrace with a sweeping view covering three regions that will take your breath away.   *Directions:* From the Roma-Firenze A1 autostrada, exit right at Orvieto.   Follow signs for Arezzo, turning on route 79 for Prodo.   Follow the winding road for 35 km past Prodo to Titignano.

FATTORIA TITIGNANO
Hosts: Giulio & Monica Fontani
Localita: Titignano
Orvieto (TR) 05010, Italy
tel: (0763) 308322
6 rooms with private bathrooms
Lire 50,000 per person half board
Breakfast and dinner served
Open all year
Some English spoken
Region: Umbria

For its perfect combination of hospitality, scenery, savory cuisine and charming accommodations, La Palazzetta ranks high on the list of favorite B&Bs. Patrizia Caracciolo and her family reside in the main villa in the complex of 17th-century stone buildings, while the farmers' quarters and animal stalls have been converted into guestrooms, each with private bathroom. The original architectural features of the buildings naturally enhance the twelve rooms, the stone interior walls, high-beamed ceilings and terracotta floors appropriately complementing the simple country antiques. A wonderfully comfortable living room with enormous fireplace and soft floral sofas invite guests to curl up with a good book. The former cattle barn is now a delightful restaurant, totally frescoed on one wall by a well-known set designer. One can dine in or out on the open veranda overlooking the rolling hills and distant swimming pool. Patrizia enthusiastically shows interested guests around her home, where several frescos of futurist painter Gerardo Dottori have been recovered (1920). *Directions:* From Todi follow signs for Orvieto, turning left at the sign for Palazzetta and proceeding for 7 km. From Orvieto, take route 448 toward Todi, watching for Palazzetta signs after the lake ends.

LA PALAZZETTA
Hosts: Patrizia Caracciolo Del Leone & family
Localita: Asproli
Todi (PG) 06059, Italy
tel: (075) 8853219 fax: (075) 8853358
12 rooms with private bathrooms
Lire 95,000 double B&B (prices seasonal)
*   minimum stay 3 days*
All meals served
Open all year
Excellent English spoken
Region: Umbria

La Dogana means customs house in Italian, and the fascinating history of this 16th-century building--which until 1870 served as the Papal customs house for travelers through the Grand Duchy of Tuscany--boasts visits from luminary artists as Michelangelo, Goethe, Byron and Stendhal. The 100-acre property belongs to young hosts Emanuele and Paola and, aside from the main villa, includes a stone farmhouse and a building near the stables across the street. In these two "extra" buildings 25 apartment-suites have been created. The guest quarters vary widely in condition, but all feature a living area, kitchen, bathroom and sleeping accommodations for two to six people. Each apartment is unique in decor, containing mixed antiques, prints, old sofas and wrought-iron beds. Up on a hillside, guests have a lovely view over Lake Trasimeno whose encircling highway is audible even from here. Although no meals are served, the Dogana is conveniently situated near Perugia, Cortona and Montepulciano, where an excellent meal is a cinch to find. *Directions:* From Perugia, take N75 toward Firenze, exiting at Tuoro. Turn left at first intersection, continuing 5 km to La Dogana on the right side of the road.

LA DOGANA
Host: Marchese Emanuele De Ferrari
Via Dogana 4
Tuoro sul Trasimeno (PG) 06069, Italy
tel: (075) 8230158 fax: (075) 8230252
25 suite-apartments
Lire 300-800,000 weekly
No meals served
Open all year
English spoken very well
Region: Umbria

Those who have fallen in love with the enchanting countryside of Tuscany but have found its roads too well-traveled should investigate the northern part of the Marches surrounding Urbino.   The scenery is magnificent, the ancient towns perfectly preserved and the ambience authentic.   The Blasi families, hard-working farmers, have dedicated themselves to balancing a productive farm with a bed and breakfast.   The brother's side of the family tends to the fields, while Amadeo, his wife Maria and their two sons see to the guests.   Three simple terracotta roofed houses make up the farm, and horses, cows, sheep and even peacocks roam the grounds.   The eight guestrooms, each with private bath, are spartan, and the decor uninspired, but the familial warmth of the hospitality, the excellent home cooking and the value are compensatory.   In the rustic dining room with red-checked tablecloths or on the windowed veranda overlooking the gently rolling, wooded countryside, guests indulge in Maria's spinach ravioli or hand-cut tagliatelle, fresh-baked bread and local wine.   *Directions:* From Urbino take the road to Urbania. Pass through town and follow signs for Acqualagna.   After 9 km turn right where indicated and follow signs up to L'Orsaiola.

L'ORSAIOLA
Hosts: The Blasi families
Localita: Orsaiola
Urbania 61049 (PS) 61049, Italy
tel: (0722) 318988/319773
8 rooms with private bathrooms
Lire 36,000 double B&B
All meals served
Open all year
No English spoken
Region: Marches

Isabella and her husband came down from the Dolomite mountains to the enchanting area surrounding the town of Urbino 20 years ago and have resided there ever since.   Their stone farmhouse is situated on the summit of one of the rolling green hills that characterize this bucolic countryside here.   Before starting the B&B, Isabella had her own esthetician business and continues to practice that trade by offering her guests facials and massages with her own natural herbal creams; hence the name Beauty Farm.   Guests are made to feel right at home at the Giuriatti's, sharing the spacious living room, well-furnished with family antiques, and dining room where meals are enjoyed all together at a big table.   As the cook is from Sardinia, specialties served are not specific to the Marches. However, one regional delicacy often figures in the dishes, since part of the farm is a white-truffle reserve.   Upstairs are found the five guestrooms, each with bath, casually and individually arranged using a mix of old and new furniture and personal family items.   Besides the beautiful university town of Urbino, other interesting sidetrips are to nearby San Leo and the Republic of San Marino. *Directions:* From Urbino (10 km) take route 73 toward Arezzo.   After Montesoffio turn right at Pozzuolo.

THE BEAUTY FARM
Host: Isabella Giuriatti
Localita: Pozzuolo 60-Montesoffio
Urbino, (PS) 61029, Italy
tel: (0722) 57183
5 rooms with private bathrooms
Lire 65,000 per person half board
Breakfast and dinner served
Open all year
English spoken well
Region: Marches

The recently opened Brombolona inn was discovered by chance in the back hills of Urbino.   Benny and his wife Lucia, natives of the area and long-time owners of the renowned "Nuovo Coppiere" restaurant in town, knew what they were doing when they purchased and painstakingly restored this 15th-century stone "castle." Perched atop a small mountain, surrounded by national park, it offers 360-degree panoramas from every window.   Gregarious Benny's dream has been realized with the completion of the inn: a home in an idyllic setting where friends old and new can visit and be assured of absolute repose.   The eighteen comfortable rooms with bath are furnished in a modern and functional fashion lacking obvious charm.   The views and Lucia's superb fresh cuisine compensate.   Truffles are the local specialty.   Benny's enthusiasm for the area is contagious and he soon has guests on outings to his favorite spots (the old mill, bell tower, abandoned convent), enhancing them with his substantial historical knowledge.   When asked how many stars his inn has, his answer is that the only stars he knows of blanket the black sky over his beloved Brombolona.   *Directions:* From Urbino (18 km) take road to Fossombrone, turn left at Brombolona sign and follow winding road to the end.

LOCANDA BROMBOLONA
Hosts: Benny & Lucia Nocoli
Localita: Sant'Andrea in Primicilio
Canavaccio di Urbino (PS) 61029, Italy
tel: (0722) 53501/320092
18 rooms with private bathrooms
Lire 75,000 double B&B
All meals served
Credit cards: all major
Open all year
English spoken well
Region: Marches

The Gasthof Obereggen, located in the Ega Valley is very simple, but its location and price are hard to match. The inn is situated on the side of a hill overlooking a gorgeous valley in one of the most beautiful mountain regions of northeastern Italy. The town of Obereggen is a ski resort and the lift is just a few minutes' walk away. From the sun-drenched deck, which extends generously out from the hotel, there is an absolutely glorious vista across the meadows to the mountains. Behind the hotel even more majestic peaks poke jaggedly into the sky. Inside there is a cozy dining room. Signor Pichler must be a hunter, for trophies line the walls, and there is a typical tiled stove against one wall to keep the room toasty on a cold day. The inn has twelve basically uninspired bedrooms, with those on the second floor opening out onto balconies with lovely views. The Gasthof's greatest asset is Signora Pichler. She is very special, running her little inn with warmth and gaiety. Signora Pichler speaks no English, but her hospitality overcomes all language barriers, and her abundant and delicious home-style cooking speaks to all who love to eat. *Directions:* Obereggen is almost impossible to find on any map, although the Val d'Ega and the town of Ega (San Floriano on some maps) are usually indicated. Obereggen is three km south of Nova Levante and 25 km southeast of Bolzano.

GASTHOF OBEREGGEN
Hosts: Pichler family
Obereggen (BZ) 39050 Val d'Ega, Italy
(Obereggen also called San Floriano)
tel: (0471) 615722
12 rooms several with private bathrooms
Lire 60,000 per person full board
All meals served
Closed April and November
No English spoken
Region: Alto Adige

At first glance the exterior of the Pensione Seguso appears quite bland: a rather boxy affair with few of the elaborate architectural enhancements so frequently evident in Venice.　Inside, however, the pension radiates warmth and charm, with oriental rugs setting off antique furniture and an heirloom silver service.　The hotel is located on the "left bank" of Venice: across the Grand Canal from the heart of the tourist area, about a 15-minute walk to St Mark's Square (or only a few minutes by ferry from the Accademia boat stop).　For several generations the hotel has been in the Seguso family, which provides a homey ambience for guests who do not demand luxury.　In front there is a miniature terrace harboring a few umbrella-shaded tables.　Several of the bedrooms have views of the canal (although these are the noisiest due to canal traffic).　Being a simple pension, most of the rooms share a bathroom, so if you are looking for hotel amenities, Seguso may not be your cup of tea.　The pleasant surprise is that the value-conscious tourist can stay here with breakfast and dinner included for the price of a room alone at most Venice hotels.　*Directions:* The Seguso is a 10-minute walk from the Accademia boat stop.

PENSIONE SEGUSO
Hosts: Seguso family
Grand Canal Zattere 779
Venice 30123, Italy
tel: (041) 5222340　fax: (041) 5222340
36 rooms, a few with private bathrooms
Lire 179,000-211,500 per person half board
Breakfast and dinner served
Open all year
English spoken well
Region: Veneto

Halfway along Lake Maggiore, at the point where the road curves back down to Verbania, is a farmhouse ideally situated 700 meters above the lake. It commands a 360-degree view which includes the Alps and Lakes Mergozzo, Monate, Varese and Maggiore with its miniature Borromeo islands (accessible by ferryboat). Just 20 km from the Swiss border, it makes a convenient and picturesque stopover on the way into or out of Italy. A 5 km km road winds up to the turn-of-the-century house with tower. Energetic and friendly hostess Iside Minotti and her family run the inn and rustic restaurant, which is busy spot in the summer when locals come up to dine and take advantage of the cooler air and the spectacular view. Menu ingredients come directly from the vegetable garden and orchards to the kitchen, where sumptuous local specialties are prepared. Even Papa Minotti gets involved and can be heard singing folk songs at the open grill. The 25-acre farm includes riding stables where guests can borrow a horse for a ride through the woods, or, for a breathtakingly scenic ride over the lake, the hotel can arrange for a helicopter from Fondotoce. Six basic and modern, though comfortable, double rooms with bath are available for overnight guests. *Directions:* Before Verbania, at Pallanza, take Via Azari to Monterosso (left turnoff) up winding road.

IL MONTEROSSO
Host: Iside Minotti
Cima Monterosso
Verbania (NO) 28048, Italy
tel: (0323) 556510
6 rooms with private bathrooms
Lire 50,000 per person half board
All meals served
Open Easter-November
Some English spoken
Region: Piedmont

With great finesse, determined partners Paolo and Andrea, an editor and a renowned chef, respectively, managed to purchase this magnificent Renaissance villa--no easy feat, considering the property had been in one family for 700 years. The pale-yellow villa with handsome lawns and surrounding cypress woods commands a spectacular view over the immense valley and Mugello mountain range. This is the area north of Florence known for its concentration of Medici villas. The 8 guestrooms have been restored to their original splendor, with high Florentine woodworked ceilings, carefully selected antiques and delightful blue-and-white-tiled bathrooms. The honeymoon suite features a grand gold-crowned red canopy bed. The entry leads directly to the frescoed dining rooms where Andrea performs his culinary magic. Original combinations of fresh local produce are served with great attention to detail, accompanied by an excellent selection of wines. Having just opened, the Villa Campestri is offering promotional rates which represent a true bargain. *Directions:* Exit at Barberino from the Bologna-Firenze A1 autostrada and head toward Borgo San Lorenzo. Continue past Sagginale, turning right for Campestri (at end of the road).

VILLA CAMPESTRI
Host: Paolo Pasquali
Localita: Campestri
Vicchio di Mugello (FI) 50039, Italy
tel: (055) 8400107   fax: (055) 8400108
8 rooms with private bathrooms
Lire 152,000 double B&B
All meals served
Credit cards: all major
Closed January and February
English spoken well
Region: Tuscany

Once you have visited La Volpaia you will understand why a young American writer who came as a guest two years ago has been living and working there ever since. This is indeed a special place, and not only for the novelist, Chris, who shares responsibility for running the place with sculptor Andrea Taliaco, a native Roman who bought and restored the 16th-century villa and farm five years ago. Guests are made to feel welcome from the moment they arrive. Ten tastefully decorated rooms, all with bath, are divided between the main house and a farmhouse down the hill at poolside, and each offers splendid views of the lush Chianti hills. The rooms are furnished with pretty country antiques and floral bedspreads and curtains. Chris tends to the nine horses, which are available for excursions into the Tuscan countryside. When guests sit down together for one of Patrizia's exquisite meals, accompanied by the Volpaia's own Chianti, conversation is never lacking. It is no wonder that guests return again and again to this idyllic spot. *Directions:* Take the superstrada north from Siena and exit at Poggibonsi, following signs for Barberino. Pass through Vico d'Elsa and turn left onto driveway indicating Volpaia.

LA VOLPAIA
Host: Andrea Taliaco
Strada di Pastine
Vico d'Elsa (FI) 50050, Italy
tel: (055) 8073063
10 rooms with private bathrooms
Lire 145,000 per person half board
Breakfast and dinner served
Open all year
Fluent English spoken
Region: Tuscany

On the northern outskirts of the beautiful city of Treviso, which combines a rich historical center with a thriving industrial base (it is home to Benetton), is a busy farm which was once a convent. The long building has been made into several residences, one belonging to the two Milani brothers, where a restaurant and six bedrooms have been fashioned for guests. All of the bedrooms have private baths, and their decor is very much in keeping with the simple country style of the farm. Typical Venetian antiques enhance the rooms, which also feature homey touches such as white-lace curtains and soft floral armchairs. Guests can observe the wine production taking place on the farm and are also welcome to take horses out on excursions, or take riding lessons if desired. The restaurant, which is popular with locals as well, prides itself on serving local specialties prepared with the farm's fresh produce and game. The bar/restaurant with its large, open central hearth, is a welcoming gathering spot, decorated with lots of pictures, brass pots, pink tablecloths and fresh flowers. *Directions:* From Venice (34 km away), take route N13 through Treviso, and on toward Villorba, turning left at the sign for the Podere.

PODERE DEL CONVENTO
Hosts: Renzo & Davide Milani
Via IV Novembre 16
Villorba (TV) 31050, Italy
tel: (0422) 92044
6 rooms with private bathrooms
Lire 75,000 double B&B
All meals served
Closed January
Very little English spoken
Region: Veneto

Sergio and Ninna Fiorentini have recently transformed the main building on their family's 300-acre tobacco farm (just 38 km from Orvieto) into a very comfortable bed and breakfast, offering visitors the opportunity to stay in the area which was once the heart of Etruscan civilization (Tarquinia, Tuscania).   Arriving guests are warmly received in the luminous, open living room furnished with antiques surrounding a grand fireplace.   Downstairs (where the livestock once dwelled) is the large, attractive restaurant overlooking the garden where guests can enjoy the fine cuisine of the Lazio region at any meal.   Or diners can opt to eat outdoors on the terrace by the saltwater pool and jacuzzi.   The four bedrooms off the courtyard of the main house have the most character and the most space, while the remaining 16, added in a cottage-like wing, are more modern in decor.   Ninna has decorated with great care, including items from her own home.   She has also worked wonders with the landscaping, which pleasingly distracts the eye from the rather bland and flat countryside surrounding Viterbo. *Directions:* From Rome (120 km away) follow signs for Viterbo. Take Cassia road north of Viterbo toward Montefiascone for four miles, turning right at Rinaldone sign.

RESIDENCE RINALDONE
Hosts: Sergio & Ninna Fiorentini
Strada Rinaldone, S.S. Cassia km 86
Viterbo 01021, Italy
tel: (0761) 3521137 fax: (0761) 250678
20 rooms with private bathrooms
Lire 110,000 double B&B
Credit cards: all major
All meals served
Open all year
English spoken well
Region: Lazio

HOTEL RESERVATION REQUEST LETTER IN ITALIAN

HOTEL NAME & ADDRESS - clearly printed or typed

Vi prego di voler riservare: I would like to request:

_____   *Numero delle camere con bagno o doccia privata*
Number of rooms with private bath or shower

_____   *Numero delle camere senza bagno o doccia*
Number of rooms without private bath or shower

_____   *Data di arrivo*   _____   *Data di Partenza*
Date of arrival   Date of departure

Vi prego inoltre de fornirmi le seguenti informazioni:
Please let me know as soon as possible the following:

Potete riservare le camere richieste?	*SI*	*NO*
Can you reserve the space requested?	yes	no

Prezzo giornaliero _____
Price per night

I pasti sono compresi nel prezzo?	*SI*	*NO*
Are meals included in your rate?	yes	no
E necessario un deposito?	SI	NO
Do you need a deposit?	yes	no

Quanto e necessario come deposito? _____
How much deposit do you need?

Ringraziando anticipatamente, porgo distinti saluti,
Thanking you in advance, I send my best regards,

YOUR NAME & ADDRESS - clearly printed or typed

Index

DISCOVERIES FROM OUR READERS

If you have a favorite hideaway that you would be willing to share with other readers, we would love to hear from you. The type of accommodations we feature are those with old world ambiance, special charm, historical interest, attractive setting, and, above all, warmth of welcome. Please send the following information:

1. *Your name, address and telephone number.*

2. *Name, address and telephone number of your discovery.*

3. *Rate for a double room including tax, service and breakfast.*

4. *Brochure or picture (we cannot return material).*

5. *Permission to use an edited version of your description.*

6. *Would you want your name, city, and state included in the book?*

Please send to:

Karen Brown's Country Inn Guides, Post Office Box 70, San Mateo, CA 94401, USA
Telephone (415) 342-5591   Fax (415) 342-9153

Karen Brown's Country Inn Guides

The Most Reliable Series on Charming Places to Stay

KAREN BROWN'S
FRENCH
Country Inns & Itineraries

UPDATED AND REVISED • SIXTH EDITION

KAREN BROWN'S
CALIFORNIA
Country Inns & Itineraries

UPDATED AND REVISED • SECOND EDITION

KAREN BROWN'S
ITALIAN
Country Inns & Itineraries

UPDATED AND REVISED • FOURTH EDITION

KAREN BROWN'S
FRENCH
Country Bed & Breakfasts

UPDATED AND REVISED • SECOND EDITION

KAREN BROWN'S
ENGLISH
Country Bed & Breakfasts

UPDATED AND REVISED • SECOND EDITION

KAREN BROWN'S
GERMAN
Country Inns & Itineraries

UPDATED AND REVISED • THIRD EDITION

KAREN BROWN'S
ITALIAN
Country Bed & Breakfasts

NEW • FIRST EDITION

KAREN BROWN'S
ENGLISH, WELSH & SCOTTISH
Country Hotels & Itineraries

UPDATED AND REVISED • SIXTH EDITION

Order Form

KAREN BROWN'S COUNTRY INN GUIDES

Please ask in your local bookstore for KAREN BROWN'S COUNTRY INN guides.
If the books you want are unavailable, you may order directly from the publisher.

—— *Austrian Country Inns & Castles (1988 edition) $6.00*
—— *California Country Inns & Itineraries $14.95*
—— *English Country Bed & Breakfasts $13.95*
—— *English, Welsh & Scottish Country Hotels & Itineraries $14.95*
—— *French Country Bed & Breakfasts $13.95*
—— *French Country Inns & Itineraries $14.95*
—— *German Country Inns & Itineraries $14.95*
—— *Irish Country Inns (1988 edition) $6.00*
—— *Italian Country Bed & Breakfasts $13.95*
—— *Italian Country Inns & Itineraries $14.95*
—— *Portuguese Country Inns & Pousadas $12.95*
—— *Scandinavian Country Inns & Manors (1987 edition) $6.00*
—— *Spanish Country Inns & Paradors $12.95*
—— *Swiss Country Inns & Chalets (1989 edition) $6.00*

Name _____ Street _____

City _____ State _____ Zip _____ tel: _____

Credit Card (Mastercard or Visa) _____ Exp: _____

Add $3.50 for the first book and .50 for each additional book for postage & packing.
California residents add 8.25% sales tax.
Indicate number of copies of each title; send form with check or credit card information to:

KAREN BROWN'S COUNTRY INN GUIDES
Post Office Box 70, San Mateo, California, 94401, U.S.A.
Tel: (415) 342-9117   Fax: (415) 342-9153

HIDDEN TREASURES OF ITALY

Bed & Breakfast Booking Service

You may conveniently reserve any of the B&Bs in this guide through the author Nicole Franchini's booking service. Simply copy (as many times as necessary) and fill out the reservation-request form on the back of this page and fax or mail it along with a $35 booking fee per B&B (refundable ONLY in the case where neither choices are available) to:

HIDDEN TREASURES OF ITALY
934 Elmwood Avenue
Wilmette, IL 60091
Telephone and Fax: (708) 853-1312
From Europe Telephone and Fax: Italy (6) 423.882

Upon confirmation of your request(s), exact rates with current exchange rate will be quoted and full prepayment by check or money order will be required within 15 days from the date of notification. After receipt of payment, a written voucher will be issued to you to present to the B&B upon arrival.

CANCELLATION AND CHANGE POLICY

We will do our best to accommodate changes in dates or B&B choice, however this can never be guaranteed. Each additional request will require a supplementary $35 booking fee.

Full refund of prepayment (excluding the booking fee) will be given up to 30 days prior to arrival date.

No refund will be made within 30 days of your arrival

Cancellation insurance is strongly recommended.

HIDDEN TREASURES OF ITALY
RESERVATION REQUEST FORM

Name(s) of traveler(s):_____   No. in party:_____

_____   No. children:_____

_____

Address:_____   Tel:_____

_____   Fax:_____

B&B name and location:_____

Second choice:_____

Type of accommodation: single_____ double_____ triple_____ apt._____

Dates desired:_____ No. of nights:_____

Meal plan: B&B_____ half board_____ full board_____ does not apply_____

Questions or Comments:

Hidden Treasures of Italy, 934 Elmwood Avenue, Wilmette IL 60091
Tel & Fax (708) 853-1312

Karen Brown's
Italian Country Inns & Itineraries

The Choice of the Discrimating Traveller to Italy

Featuring the Finest Places to Stay with Charm, and
Detailed Itineraries for Exploring the Countryside

Italian Country Inns & Itineraries is the perfect companion guide to Karen Brown's *Italian Country Bed & Breakfasts*. Whereas the Bed & Breakfast guide has "hand-picked" the choice places to stay in private homes, the *Italian Country Inns & Itineraries* book features accommodations with great charm in small hotels and inns. All the pertinent information is given: description of the accommodation, sketch, price, driving directions, maps, if there is a restaurant, owner's name, telephone and fax number, dates open, etc.

Italian Country Inns & Itineraries does not replace *Italian Country Bed & Breakfasts* - together they make the perfect pair for the traveller who wants to explore the countryside of Italy. Both feature places to stay with charm, warmth of welcome, and old world ambiance: *Italian Country Bed & Breakfasts* features places to stay in private homes: *Italian Country Inns & Itineraries* features small hotels and inn *plus* the added bonus of five itineraries, handy for use with the Bed & Breakfast guide. Each book uses the same maps so it is easy to choose a combination of places to stay from each, adding a rich variety of choices for where to spend the night.

KAREN BROWN wrote her first travel guide, *French Country Inns & Chateaux*, in 1979. This original guide is now in its 6th edition plus 13 books have been added to the series which has become known as the most personalized, reliable reference library for the discriminating traveller. Although Karen's staff has expanded, she is still involved in the publication of her guide books. Karen, her husband, Rick, their daughter, Alexandra, and son, Richard, live on the coast south of San Francisco at their own country inn, Seal Cove Inn, in Moss Beach, California.

NICOLE FRANCHINI, author of *Italian Country Bed & Breakfasts*, was born in Chicago and raised in a bilingual family, her father having been born in Italy. She received a B.A. degree in languages from William Smith College and the Sorbonne, Paris, and has been residing in Italy for the past six years. Currently living in Rome, she runs her own travel consulting business, Hidden Treasures of Italy, which organizes specialized group and individual itineraries. Nicole also represents several hotels and bed and breakfasts in Italy.

ELISABETTA FRANCHINI, the talented artist responsible for the cover painting and illustrations in *Italian Country Bed & Breakfasts*, lives in her hometown of Chicago where she paints predominantly European landscapes and architectural scenes. This year, on her annual trip abroad, she enjoyed touring Italy with her sister, Nicole Franchini, for their collaborative Bed & Breakfast research for this guide. A Smith College graduate in Art History and French Literature, Elisabetta has exhibited extensively in the Chicago area for the past six years.

SEAL COVE INN - LOCATED IN THE SAN FRANCISCO AREA

Karen (Brown) Herbert is best known as a writer and publisher of the Karen Brown's Country Inn guides, favorites of travellers searching for the most charming country inns throughout Europe and California. Now Karen and her husband, Rick, have put sixteen years of experience into reality and opened their own superb hideaway, Seal Cove Inn. Spectacularly set amongst wildflowers and bordered by towering cypress trees, Seal Cove Inn looks out to the ocean over acres of county park: an oasis where you can enjoy secluded beaches, explore tide-pools, watch frolicking seals, and follow the tree-lined path tracing the windswept ocean bluffs. Country antiques, lovely original watercolors, flower-filled cradles, rich fabrics, and the gentle ticking of grandfather clocks create the perfect ambiance for a foggy day in front of the crackling log fire. Each bedroom is its own private haven with a comfortable sitting area before a wood-burning fireplace and doors opening onto a private patio with views to the distant ocean. Moss beach is a 30-minute drive south of San Francisco, 6 miles north of the picturesque town of Half Moon Bay, and a few minutes from Princeton harbor with its colorful fishing boats and restaurants. Seal Cove Inn makes a perfect base for whale-watching expeditions, salmon-fishing excursions, day trips to San Francisco, exploring the coast, or, best of all, just a romantic interlude by the sea - time to relax and be pampered. Karen and Rick are looking forward to meeting and welcoming you to their own inn.

Seal Cove Inn, 221 Cypress Avenue, Moss Beach, California, 94038, U.S.A.
telephone: (415) 728-7325   fax: (415) 728-4116